Catherine Clark Kroeger
& Nancy Nason-Clark

No Place
for Abuse

Biblical &
Practical Resources
to Counteract
Domestic Violence

InterVarsity Press
Downers Grove, Illinois

InterVarsity Press
P.O. Box 1400, Downers Grove, IL 60515-1426
World Wide Web: www.ivpress.com
E-mail: mail@ivpress.com

InterVarsity Press® is the book-publishing division of InterVarsity Christian Fellowship/USA®, a student
movement active on campus at hundreds of universities, colleges and schools of nursing in the United States of
America, and a member movement of the International Fellowship of Evangelical Students. For information about
local and regional activities, write Public Relations Dept., InterVarsity Christian Fellowship/USA, 6400
Schroeder Rd., P.O. Box 7895, Madison, WI 53707-7895.

Scripture quotations, unless otherwise noted, are from the New Revised Standard Version of the Bible, copyright
1989 by the Division of Christian Education of the National Council of the Churches of Christ in the USA. Used
by permission. All rights reserved.

Cover photograph © Gentl & Hyers/Photonica

ISBN 0-8308-2295-X

Printed in the United States of America ∞

Library of Congress Cataloging-in-Publication Data

Kroeger, Catherine Clark.
   No place for abuse: biblical & practical resources to counteract domestic violence/
   Catherine Clark Kroeger & Nancy Nason-Clark.
      p.   cm.
   Includes bibliographical references.
   ISBN 0-8308-2295-X (pbk.: alk. paper)
   1. Church work with problem families. 2. Family violence—Religious
aspects—Christianity. I. Nason-Clark, Nancy, 1956- II. Title.
   BV4438.5 .K76 2001
   261.8'327—dc 21
                                                              00—54447

19   18   17   16   15   14   13   12   11   10   9   8   7   6   5   4   3   2

16   15   14   13   12   11   10   09   08   07   06   05   04   03   02   01

CONTENTS

Preface

A flourishing evangelical church was enjoying a vibrant ministry, a growing membership and a powerful witness to the community. Then, rather suddenly, the pastor resigned.[1] His wife had left him. The congregation was thrown into turmoil, and the questions began. What could have happened? How could she leave when so much was being accomplished in the church? Hadn't she seen how many new people had been drawn to the church or were being discipled into fuller commitment? Had the pastor fallen into some form of sexual indiscretion or moral failure?

Little by little, rumors surfaced that the marriage had been abusive; but many church people refused to believe that this could possibly be true. Perhaps it was a smokescreen to cover up something else. Suspicions grew. A number of members withdrew from the congregation. Much blame was heaped on the one woman in whom the pastor's wife had confided. Her advice must have been faulty, went the reasoning. She must be responsible for the dissolution of the marriage and the resulting catastrophe that had befallen the church.

In the final analysis, who was to blame? The pastor who had been secretly abusing his wife for many years? The wife who refused to suffer in silence any longer? The elders who might have been more sensitive to the needs of the family? The seminary where this pastor received his training? The denomination that ordained him? The congregation that had grown to appreciate this family and their ministry? Who exactly was to blame?

Ultimately the blame is widespread, for Christian believers worldwide tend to ignore, minimize and deny the abuse that is rampant in families of faith. Churches provide few resources for victims of abuse.

Moreover, believers are discouraged from using available community services such as shelters, counseling, abusers' groups, restraining orders and legal aid. Without such help, the abuse frequently grows more severe. The potential of emotional and spiritual healing is sacrificed to silence. Silence of the sacred. *Sacred silence.*

❊   ❊   ❊

The response was a standing ovation! At a general assembly of the World Evangelical Fellowship, an African woman rose and asked, "When will this organization address violence against women? There are men in this very room who abuse their wives."

God's people were ready to examine the great wound in the churches and ready to apply the healing balm of Gilead. The Women's Commission of the WEF was asked to form a task force[2] on violence against women and to consider how the evangelical church worldwide could offer compassion and healing to victims. What is the extent of the problem of abuse? How are evangelical churches responding to the suffering caused by violence in the home? What theological principles can help the church offer hope in the midst of crises, to families both inside and outside the fold?

We can no longer afford to be indifferent to the need or to our responsibility to take appropriate action. In the first place, God's honor is at stake. Abusive marriage cannot possibly mirror Christ's love for the church. Second, the peace of the church is at stake. If there is violence in our homes, we cannot have tranquillity in the church. Further, we are failing Christian leaders and people alike. We have failed to provide guidance and correction where it is most needed, in families of faith and among families of church leaders. We have failed the victims and we have failed their oppressors. We have not sought to offer the healing of Gilead or the justice God demands.

The International Task Force began its work by developing a theological statement concerning abuse and a series of principles to reveal how God has spoken out about violence through Scripture. We were asked to write a book-length statement addressing the prevalence of abuse, together with a sustained biblical argument condemning violence and with practical strategies for churches as they respond to the needs of victims and their families.

Nancy offers the expertise of a trained sociologist; Catherine, the insights of a biblical scholar. Together we bring a variety of perspectives to bear on this complex problem. We are citizens of two different nations, trained in different disciplines on two sides of the Atlantic, born in different generations, worshiping in different evangelical traditions. But we share a united conviction that Christian churches today must recognize and respond to the suffering created by family violence.

Over the last ten years Nancy has been conducting workshops and offering training related to abuse in both religious and secular gatherings. In these contexts, she is frequently asked why there are so few resources available to help pastors and laypeople respond to the myriad needs of victims of violence and their perpetrators. Sometimes anonymous calls are left on her home office answering machine after a church speaking engagement. "When are you going to address domestic violence in clergy homes?" the nameless voices ask. When will God's people answer this plea?

In response, the first four chapters of our book will demonstrate the prevalence of violence worldwide and its presence in evangelical homes. Until we catch a glimpse of scenes of horror from around the world, we will never have eyes to see violence in the neighborhoods where we live and the churches that we attend. It is always more difficult to deal with shame in one's own backyard.

Secular knowledge alone is insufficient. Women and men alike voice another concern. When will people talk about abuse in theological language? When will they tell us what the Bible says? When will the church speak to people of faith about matters of abuse in the home? When will Christians heed the message of Scripture and begin to obey its principles? To address this need, nine chapters will present biblical reasons that Christians must acknowledge the global crisis of abuse against women. We argue that believers must respond to this evil wherever it occurs, inside or beyond the fold of faith.

Our goal is to present sociological evidence and biblical insights to challenge the church to stand up in opposition to violence against women. The early pages of the book demonstrate the prevalence and

severity of abuse in all corners of the world, among all people groups
and within all categories of believers. Chapters three and four offer
the reader tools and strategies for naming the violence in our midst
and responding compassionately to its victims. Together these chapters argue that God's house is no place for violence; our homes are *no
place for abuse*. Women and men stirred by God's love need to speak
out; hearts moved by compassion need to respond. Indeed our world
is no place for abuse.

As noted, the following nine chapters present a sustained biblical
argument condemning violence, calling believers to see afresh the
power and potential of change inherent in the Christian message of
hope. But how can this message of hope and healing from abuse be
translated into the weekly routine of church life? We close the book
with practical guidelines for congregations and resources for pastors.
Ranging from a sermon outline on abuse to questions that might guide
an interview with a battered woman, our appendices deal with practical suggestions about what individuals, pastors and churches should
know and what they can do—within the pastoral study where counseling occurs, and at the congregational level in youth events,
women's Bible studies and Sunday services. Working in unison,
churches and their leaders can combat violence against women and
proclaim the message of hope and healing.

This book is intended to speak to persons holding differing views
on the dynamics of marriage and family life. There is no room for gender politics. Abuse is wrong whether one is an egalitarian, a comple-
mentarian or a traditionalist. The time has come for believers to unite
our efforts and obey God's command to deliver the oppressed from
the hand of the violent. We need to be faithful in remonstrating with
oppressors and seeking to guide them into new patterns of behavior.
We must be tender in the care of those who are afflicted. The healing
balm of Gilead needs to be applied.

The Bible consistently calls for God's judgment on those who use
their power to inflict suffering on others. Conversely, great blessing is
promised to those who use their power to alleviate the oppression and
suffering of others. How will we—God's people—respond to this
challenge?

For too long sacred and secular caregivers have worked in isolation from one another. By blending sociological studies and biblical insights, this book sounds a call of compassion and justice to God's people around the world. As you read our book, it will become clear that it is written in two different voices—our voices, separate and distinct, but of common purpose and vision.

❖   ❖   ❖

We need to acknowledge helpful companions in our journey of writing this book. Nancy wants to thank the Louisville Institute for the Study of Protestantism and American Culture for ongoing support of her research program on Violence Against Women and Contemporary Christianity, and the Muriel McQueen Fergusson Centre for Family Violence Research at the University of New Brunswick, under whose umbrella the Religion and Violence Research Team operates. Over the last ten years over a thousand women and men, laity and clergy alike, have opened their lives to her research team and shared from their hearts about violence. Thank you for the privilege of listening to your pain and your hope. Barbara Fisher Townsend has worked diligently as Nancy's research assistant, helped on occasion by Christy Hoyt and Lenora Sleep; all of these women brighten the halls of the Department of Sociology, which houses Nancy's working space and pays indirectly for her bread and butter. David Clark, a clinical psychologist and depression researcher, continues to be her soulmate and *encourager* extraordinaire, and her children, Natascha and Christina, are still young enough to come to her home office asking for hugs, but old enough to pray that God would grant their mother wisdom and time.

There are many to whom Catherine Kroeger must express gratitude—victims, shelter workers, pastors, laypeople, counselors, leaders of batterers' groups, therapists, law enforcement personnel and even batterers. She is grateful to them for telling their stories and those of their friends—for revealing their spiritual struggles, the responses they were given by churches and individuals, and their soul-wracking questions about human agony and biblical teaching. We have sought to share their perspectives while protecting their identity, to let others know what evangelicals suffer and what they perpetrate. These nameless stalwarts have led us to look at the Bible more closely and ultimately to dare to voice our convictions.

Together, we are grateful to James Hoover of InterVarsity Press for endorsing a book that addresses evangelicals around the world about a very unpopular subject. We thank God that Jim could understand the importance of sharing the devastating truth as well as the resources that are available for healing. We also thank Winnie Bartel and the other members of the World Evangelical Task Force for their ongoing vision, assistance and encouragement. We hope you will be pleased by our efforts on your behalf.

> *Creator God:*
> *We ask, O Lord,*
> *that you would open our eyes to see*
> *the suffering of women around the world.*
> *Give us ears to hear their cries*
> *and hearts that will not rest*
> *until we have done our part*
> *to apply the healing balm of Gilead*
> *to their wounds.*
> *Amen.*

1

The Prevalence
& Severity of Abuse
Against Women

O ur purpose in writing this book is to challenge the evangelical
Christian community to listen to the voices of women from
around the world—including their own backyard—talk about
the violence they have suffered. We want to address the problem
straightforwardly: to offer information so that church people and pastors will be ignorant no longer, to offer advice on effective biblical ways
to respond to victims and their families, and then to offer a challenge
that congregations and their leaders take up positions among community and national groups committed to eliminating violence in our midst,
encouraging violence-free family living, and responding with the mind
and heart of Christ to those who suffer violence.

Christians should not be ill-informed about the nature, prevalence
and severity of abuse that characterizes our churches, our neighborhoods and our world. We believe that most Christian people, when
provided with both the biblical teaching condemning violence and
social science data about its consequences, will want to do something

about it. We do not believe that the Spirit-filled life should include abusive acts, nor should it turn a blind eye to the suffering of another.

Violence against women is a reality. It exists in every country of the globe, among all people groups. Abuse occurs within every faith community. And it knows no socioeconomic boundaries. Rich women, poor women, black women, white women, educated women, illiterate women, religious women, beautiful women—all women are potential targets of violence, and all women are at some degree of risk.

> In a study of women in Britain, up to 25 percent of women reported having experienced physical abuse at the hands of an intimate partner. Violence was associated with increased rates of miscarriage, premature birth, low birth weight and fetal injury, including fetal death.
> (Mezey and Bewley 1997; <www.jhuccp.org/popline/psm/feb00.stm>)

Governments around the world are recognizing the devastating consequences of violence against women, and researchers and health care professionals are being called upon for expert advice and guidance for both community-level actions (like emergency response teams) and national policy initiatives. Large sums of money are now being directed toward research on the elimination of violence, reforming the judicial system to respond to the needs of victims and perpetrators,[1] and ensuring that health and other social services offer effective coordinated responses to the needs of abused women and their dependent children.

There is immense documentation, from academic researchers, women's organizations, policy analysts, health care providers and victim support groups, of the prevalence and severity worldwide of violence against women and the girl child. Since 1995 and the Beijing Conference, many nation-states have sought to take seriously the challenge to reduce women's risk of physical or sexual assault. Professional organizations like the Association of Physicians and Gynecologists have responded with protocols for their members, and umbrella organizations like the World Health Organization have held consultations, created task forces, produced training materials and conducted research among their member groups. The

World Bank has documented the enormous cost of violence. Some political parties in power, or in opposition, have sought to address violence against women through policy statements, zero tolerance declarations, directives, government grants and community initiatives.

Amid growing world recognition of the problems women face, everyday fears, the bruises and battering they experience, and the needs of their children for safety and security, where are the churches? Why have religious groups been so slow to recognize violence against women and so slow to respond to victims' cries for help? Indeed, amid the ever-increasing number of men and women worldwide who recognize the severity of woman abuse and have personal and professional

> Canadian women with a violent father-in-law are at three times the risk for spouse abuse as women with a non-violent father-in-law. (Statistics Canada 1993 Violence Against Women Survey)

commitment to work toward its elimination, where are God's people, called in God's name to bring healing in the midst of suffering?

By and large, a "holy hush"[2] pervades religious organizations. Violence is ugly, and most churches and their leaders feel uncomfortable talking about it and ill-equipped to respond to its victims. The issue is very sensitive, and many people and pastors alike would prefer to sweep it under the proverbial church carpet. Moreover, violence touches many people at the core of their being, because they either recognize in themselves the tendency to control others or have suffered humiliation at the hands of someone else.

Let's face our reluctance head-on: the reality and consequences of violence make most Christian people—indeed most any people anywhere—very uncomfortable. As the people of God, we would prefer to think abuse does not occur in our churches' families. So we act as if it were someone else's problem, something we do not need to contend with ourselves.

But violence is everyone's problem. It is an issue that is not going away. It is prevalent in our churches and in the communities our churches serve. We need to crawl out from under the church carpet and admit that we have been hiding from the problem, sometimes contributing to it, and not very committed to being part of its solution.

Many voices declare that the church has either caused men to be violent toward their wives or at least provided fertile soil for men's mistreatment of power within their families. They argue that since the church is part of the problem, it cannot be part of the solution. Thus when violence against women is being discussed, God's people are seldom consulted. Since we speak out so infrequently about violence, our collective voice is never heard on this issue. Generally speaking, leaders in religious organizations and those involved in community pastoral care are never even invited to participate at the secular consultation table. The silence of our churches and our leaders is often interpreted in the public square as complicity with violent acts.

It is assumed—we think erroneously—that Christian people do not have a biblical response to the suffering of women worldwide. It is assumed—we think erroneously—that the healing journey of a victim has nothing to do with her walk of faith. It is assumed—we think erroneously—that pastoral care has nothing unique to offer and could be damaging to a woman's search for health and wholeness.

The time has come to challenge the contemporary evangelical church to wake up to the prevalence of violence in its midst, to take up its role as part of a community-based response, and to offer the healing balm of Gilead to those who suffer the devastating consequences of abuse. Men and women filled with devotion to God can play a vital role in proclaiming this message: every home a safe place, every home a shelter. There is no place like home. When abuse strikes, there is no home.

As we enter a new millennium, we believe the time has come for a renewed prophetic voice to emerge from the pew and from behind the pulpit—voices that want to change our communities, challenge our people, and to offer new strategies to ensure that our world is a safer place in which to live. Christian people ought to be men and women of hope and of vision—binding up the broken-hearted and showing all people everywhere a more excellent way. It is in that spirit of hope that we share our vision—a vision where the evangelical church worldwide would join hands to condemn all types of abuse, to recognize in particular the suffering of women, and its consequences for children, and to commit our time and our passion to work toward the elimination of all forms of family violence—with God as our guide, Jesus as our companion, and the Holy Spirit as our comforter. We need God's direction, the companionship and blessed example of Christ, and the Spirit to both strengthen us in the struggle and to apply the healing balm. In the pages to follow, we present the data (individual narratives and national statistics), followed by the challenge to change the world, one home at a time. Let us not forget, *the home is no place for abuse.*

Woman Abuse in the Church

Statistics are an important component in the story of abuse worldwide. Narrative accounts of the lives of ordinary women give context to those statistics, enabling researcher and reader alike to visualize real women living in a specific time and a specific place amid very real problems. Later on we will present quantitative data gathered from large-scale studies from many of the major countries of the world. These reveal the extent of violence against women in every corner of the globe. But first we present accounts of the lives of four women, all evangelical Christians, all victims of violence. Their stories reveal several pieces of the puzzle, component parts of a complex web of faith, family, fear and violence. As in all the stories told in this book, names and identifying information have been changed to protect the identity of the women; the details of their abuse, however, have not been altered.

> One in four women in Latin America is a victim of physical abuse; 20 percent of women's work absenteeism is the direct result of violence in the home. (<www.saartjie.co.za/march2000/vaw14.htm>)

Janice and her family moved to Sydney, Australia, from western Europe when she was a child. Her missionary parents settled into a nomadic existence, working among aboriginal peoples. In time she met a newly converted aboriginal man, and some years later they were married. With a thriving ministry, life was very exciting for them.

An unplanned pregnancy, though, began to exacerbate some of Janice's husband's problems with anger. Whenever he got angry, he hit her. Janice knew there was a cultural component to her abuse, for often she had bathed wounds of aboriginal women who had been battered by their husbands.

Before long a six-week cycle developed: calm, growing discontent, violent outbursts, an apology—and the cycle began again. Life was growing very difficult for Janice, she suffered a cracked skull from beatings to the head and broken ribs from blows to the chest.

Authorities within the hierarchy of their denomination were called to give counsel. There was much prayer but no firm reprimand for the husband's violent ways. On one occasion Janice gathered up her six children and fled her home, fearing he was going to kill her. Eventually he was temporarily removed from church leadership when his threat to murder her was voiced in front of influential church leaders.

While her husband is no longer in pastoral leadership and the frequency and severity of the violence have begun to decline, Janice has never received the supportive services she needed from either local police or community organizations, and the church family too has let her down. The violence she suffered has never been condemned, nor has healing been offered to her broken body and spirit.[3]

Macy had a heart for God and had worked in a Christian mission organization most of her adult life. Trained as a nurse and later as an administrator, she felt moved by suffering around the world and responded by offering her time and her talents. For years Macy struggled with depression and low self-esteem. Finally she decided she needed to find a more caring church family, to help address some of her malaise and offer her more opportunities to use her gifts.

Macy was drawn to a small fellowship with a set of programs for seniors in low-cost housing. She quickly established herself as a hard worker and a committed follower of Christ. Before long the pastor and his wife, both in their fifties, took a special interest in her life. But the pastor's interest developed in ways both unanticipated and unwelcomed. He engaged in sexual indiscretions with her, then weeks later raped her, taking advantage of her loneliness and the emotional vulnerability she had expressed to him during counseling sessions. Because he was highly respected in the community, no one was willing to believe her story of sexual abuse, and no one offered to help her seek healing and wholeness in its aftermath.[4]

The stories of Janice and Macy exemplify violence against Christian women around the globe. No multinational studies have collected statistics *specifically* on the prevalence of woman abuse among evangelical believers. But as we shall see, there is growing evidence that violence is all too common an experience in the life of women believers within ordinary evangelical and mainstream churches.

What we do know is that violence against Christian women has impact on the spiritual journeys of individual women and their families, and often on the life of the congregations to which they belong. While abuse may be committed behind closed doors, its shock waves extend well beyond the family context. Like their secular sisters who have been battered, religious victims of abuse bear the scars of physical and emotional pain. Janice's physical and emotional abuse and Macy's sexual abuse have brought long-term consequences for both women, their ministries and their families. But their pain has spiritual overtones as well. Each woman has been silenced by elders in her faith tradition. Each woman has learned that her spiritual leaders care more about the reputation of the abuser than the scars of the abused. When each woman gathered the courage to tell her story of betrayal, she was dismissed by those who might have helped to chart her healing journey.

In *Domestic Violence: What Every Pastor Needs to Know*, the Reverend Al Miles says that two themes emerged from his nonrandom survey of over one hundred pastors: the importance they attach to saving marriages at all costs and the pastoral temptation toward quick-fix solutions for abusive men and abused women.[5]

In a small study of 187 American women who qualified as being abuse-free for at least one year, Anne Horton, Melany Wilkins and Wendy Wright found that 54 percent of religious victims and 38 percent of nonreligious victims sought help from a religious professional in the aftermath of violence in the home.[6]

During the fall of 1989, the Christian Reformed Church in North America conducted a survey among a random sample of one thousand adult members attending their churches. Of the 643 responses they received, 28 percent had experienced at least one form of abuse. A total of 12 percent reported physical abuse, 13 percent sexual abuse, and 19 percent emotional abuse; as these numbers reveal, many had experienced more than one form of abuse. Converting these prevalence rates to the actual number of people victimized, the Christian Reformed Church estimates that between forty-eight and sixty-two thousand adult members have experienced physical, sexual or emotional abuse.

A research initiative involving evangelical clergy in the Atlantic Provinces of Canada[7] revealed that pastors perceive violence rates among married couples in their current congregation to be 19 percent, just under one in five.[8] These same pastors estimate the rate of violence in the secular culture to be about 29 percent, a full ten percentage points higher than in their congregations. This is despite the fact that researchers in the field of family violence have consistently argued that abuse crosses all religious boundaries and that the rates inside and outside the walls of the church are similar.

In Romania, 29 percent of women between fifteen and fifty-five who sought treatment at the Bucharest Forensic Hospital were beaten by an intimate partner; of these, 87 percent had been assaulted by an instrument that pierced the skin. (<www.wave-network.org/articles/486.htm>)

Violence among families of faith reflects the cultures they inhabit, but interweaving the narrative is their faith and religious identity. The role of religion in helping women find their voice is both curious and critical. Macy and Janice had the courage to speak the words that name their experience, though their cries for help fell on deaf ears. Some women do not live long enough to disclose their abuse, and others are prevented by a lack of social, economic and religious power.

Susan Pickles never had the chance to tell her story. Death robbed her of life and a voice. But just one year ago, an American paper told the details of her death to the world. Scott Pickles, a former lawyer in his early forties, took the lives of his wife and two children in New London, Connecticut. According to the *Norwich Bulletin* of October 28, 1999, the guilty man, a born-again believer, apologized in court to the victim's family, his family and his clients. But his remorse could not bring three dead bodies back to life. Apparently Pickles was experiencing severe debt, limited professional success and fear that his wife would leave him. In a final act of control, he had determined their fate.

Before Pickles was handcuffed and taken away, the father of the slain woman asked the judge to deliver a message to the man who killed his daughter and grandchildren, "Tell him I don't hate him . . . I do forgive him." With his voice cracking, the elderly man gazed heavenward and said that he would look forward to joining his slain family members—all of whom were evangelical Christians—someday in heaven.

For many American Christians, it is inconceivable that an evangelical man in their country would be found guilty of murdering his wife and children. For many nonevangelicals, it is inconceivable that the father of a slain woman and grandfather of two slain grandchildren would want to give a message of forgiveness to the murderer. Most people around the globe would find it hard to understand why someone with so many resources and opportunities at his fingertips would feel so hopeless. It is a multilayered story, to be sure—the desperation, the control, the faith and the consequences. As we shall see in later chapters, the issue of forgiveness is central to understanding the complexity of the relationship between religion, abuse and the healing journey.

According to Anne Horton and Judith Williamson in *Abuse and Religion: When Praying Isn't Enough*, more abuse victims, perpetrators and family members seek help from ordained ministers and other religious leaders than from all other helping professionals combined.[9] In 1988 Lee Bowker reported the results of two studies of religious abuse victims and the help they reported receiving from ordained ministers. One-third of the women who responded to his survey in *Woman's Day* magazine reported that they had been the recipient of some form of pastoral counsel; in terms of effectiveness, the women rated the assistance from clergy as less helpful than that from other sources of support.[10]

Vimla's story was told only to a researcher; otherwise it was sheltered from public knowledge by secrecy, shame and silence. Vimla is the wife of an evangelist, a man who travels throughout southeastern Asia spreading the gospel. They met at a church youth gathering when they were both in their teens. According to Vimla, they married out of love, feeling an initial attraction to each other and the sense that God would bless their home. During the early years of their marriage, Vimla reports, her husband was very kind, and during this time she bore him two sons and one daughter. His ministry began to flourish, but his treatment of his own family began to deteriorate. For several years Vimla has been the victim of repeated beatings. "He is very kind and good to people outside the home, but not to us," she confides. "Somehow he does not beat me up in the presence of our children, which I appreciate." She feels frightened and very alone.[11]

While there are many features in common between Vimla's life and the lives of battered religious women in other contexts, there is a cultural reality that we need to consider. Recently four hundred evangelical women participated in data gathering in India and other parts of Asia concerning woman abuse. Three of every four women reported some form of physical abuse by their husbands. Women whose marriages were arranged by parents were less likely to report physical violence. One reason for this seems to be the level of involvement by the extended family when a marriage is arranged.[12]

In an informal discussion session held in India among religious leaders from many faith communities and a variety of nations, it was disclosed that one reason Asian men beat their wives is that men do not like women to be assertive or articulate or to answer back to their husbands or other elders in the family.[13] While the cultural contexts vary, the devastating consequences bear a marked similarity: the body is harmed, emotions are damaged, the relationship dies and the spirit is crushed.

As we consider statistics from countries around the globe, let us remember the lives of Janice, Macy, Susan and Vimla representing evangelical women, some with voice, some without voice, bearing the marks of violence and suffering its consequences.

Woman Abuse Across the World
Violence against women is a worldwide problem. Although abuse takes many forms, happens in many places and affects women differently, the first step in understanding the magnitude of the problem is

to look at its frequency. Researchers from all corners of the globe have demonstrated that domestic violence threatens the physical and mental health and security of millions of women. A woman living in the First World *or* the developing world is more likely to be injured, raped or physically threatened by a current or former intimate partner than by a stranger or any other person. That is why many women's organizations have claimed that violence is the number-one fear or reality of women worldwide.

The statistics are startling. Violence against women is a pervasive problem in North America, Europe, Africa, Asia and South America. In every country where woman abuse has been studied using a large-scale sample and consistent measures, at least one in ten women reports that she has been physically abused by an intimate male partner, such as a husband or ex-husband. These figures *do not* include verbal abuse, sexual assault or threats of violence. As such they are very conservative estimates of violence against women. Moreover, data like these rely on women's self-reports of victimization. The abuse of women who are unwilling to admit to themselves what has happened, or unwilling to disclose their pain to an outsider, simply goes unreported.

> One in every four South African women is assaulted by her boyfriend or husband every week. (UN Children's Emergency Fund, quoted in *YOU* magazine, January 26, 1995)

Physical abuse includes behaviors such as kicking, biting and punching. Sometimes an object is used to inflict harm, such as a knife or gun. It is not uncommon for women to sustain serious injuries at the hands of a partner; sometimes they die as a result of abuse. All victimized women feel shame, betrayal and fear. Some try to hide the secret of their abuse; others gather up enough courage to escape.

As table 1 reveals, in every country where reliable data has been collected, large numbers of women have been physically assaulted by a male intimate partner. When the referent point is physical assault by a male intimate during the last twelve months, at least one in every five women (20 percent) in Australia, Chile, Korea, Nicaragua, Peru, Rwanda, and the West Bank and Gaza Strip responds in the affirmative. When the referent point is during the course of the relationship

Table 1. Violence Against Women Around the World

Country	Year of study	Sample size	Percentage of adult women who have been physically assaulted by an intimate partner[14]	Publication information
AUSTRALIA (Metro Melbourne)	1993-1994	1,494	22.4% in past 12 months	Mazza et al. 1996
AUSTRALIA (national)	1996	6,300	23.0% ever assaulted by a spouse 2.6% in past 12 months	McLennan 1996
BANGLA-DESH (national villages)	1992	1,225	19.0% in past 12 months 47.0% ever in any relationship	Schuler et al. 1996
CAMBODIA (six provinces and Phnom Penh)	1995	1,374	16% by current spouse	Nelson and Zimmerman 1996
CANADA (national)	1993	12,300	3.0% in past 12 months 29.0% ever in any relationship	Rodgers 1994; *Statistics Canada* 1993
CANADA (Toronto)	1991-1992	420	27.4% ever in any relationship	Randall et al. 1995
CHILE (Metro Santiago & Santiago Prov.)	1993	1,000	26.0% in current relationship	Larrain-Heiremans 1993
CHILE (Santiago)	1997	310	22.5% in past 12 months	Morrison et al. 1997
COLOMBIA (national)	1995	6,097	19.3% ever in any relationship	DHS 1995
EGYPT (national)	1995-1996	7,121	34.4% ever in any relationship	DHS 1995
ENGLAND (national)	1996	6,000	23.0% ever assaulted by a spouse 4.2% in last 12 months	British Crime Survey 1996; Mirrlees-Black 1999
ETHIOPIA (Meskanena Woreda)	1995	673	10.0% in past 12 months 45.0% ever in any relationship	Deyessa et al. 1998

Table 1—*Continued* 25

Country	Year of study	Sample size	Percentage of adult women who have been physically assaulted by an intimate partner[14]	Publication information
INDIA (rural areas in 2 states)	1993-1994	1,842	40.0% in current relationship	Jejeebhoy 1997
KENYA (Kisii District)	1984-1987	612	42.0% in current relationship	Raikes 1990
MALAYSIA (national)	1989	713	39.0% in past 12 months	Women's Aid Organization 1992
MEXICO (Durango City)	1996	384	40.0% ever in any relationship	Alvarado-Zaldivar et al. 1998
MEXICO (Metropolitan Guadalajara)	1996	650	15.0% in past 12 months	Ramirez et al. 1996
NETHER-LANDS (national)	1986	1,016	20.8% ever in any relationship	Römkens 1997
NICARAGUA (León)	1993	360	27.0% in past 12 months	Ellsberg 1997
NICARAGUA (Managua)	1997	378	30.2% in past 12 months	Morrison et al. 1997
NIGERIA (not stated)	1993	1,000	31.4% ever in any relationship	Odujinrin 1993
NORWAY (Trondheim)	1989	111	18.0% ever in any relationship	Schei 1989
PAPUA NEW GUINEA (national; Port Moresby; low income)	1984	298	56.1% ever in any relationship	Centro Paraguayo de Estudios de Población 1996
PAPUA NEW GUINEA (national; rural)	1982	628	67.0% ever in any relationship	Bradley 1988
PARAGUAY (western state, except Chaco)	1995-1996	6,465	9.5% ever in any relationship	Centro Paraguayo de Estudios de Población 1996
PERU (Metropolitan Lima)	1997	359	30.9% in past 12 months	Gonzales et al. 1997

Table 1—*Continued*

Country	Year of study	Sample size	Percentage of adult women who have been physically assaulted by an intimate partner[14]	Publication information
PHILIPPINES (national)	1993	8,481	5.1% ever in any relationship	DHS 1994
PUERTO RICO (national)	1993-1996	7,079	12.8% ever in any relationship	Departamento de Salud y la Escuela 1998
RWANDA (Kigali)	1990	874	21.0% in past 12 months	van der Straten et al. 1995
SOUTH AFRICA (Eastern Cape)	1998	403	10.9% in past 12 months 26.8% ever in any relationship	Jewkes et al. 1999
SOUTH AFRICA (Mpumalanga)	1998	428	11.9% in past 12 months 28.4% ever in any relationship	Macro Int'l and South Africa Department of Health 1999
SOUTH AFRICA (Northern Province)	1998	475	45% in past 12 months 19.1% ever in any relationship	Jewkes et al. 1999
SWITZER-LAND (national)	1994-1996	1,500	6.3% in past 12 months 12.6% ever in any relationship	Gillioz et al. 1996
THAILAND (Bangkok)	1994	619	20.0% in current relationship	Hoffman et al. 1994
TURKEY (East and Southeast Anatolia)	1998	599	57.9% ever in any relationship	Ilkkaracan et al. 1998
UGANDA (Lira and Masaka districts)	1995-1996	1,660	40.5% in current relationship	Blanc et al. 1996
UNITED KINGDOM (North London)	1993	430	12.0% in past 12 months 30.0% ever in any relationship	Mooney 1993

Table 1—*Continued* 27

Country	Year of study	Sample size	Percentage of adult women who have been physically assaulted by an intimate partner[14]	Publication information
UNITED STATES OF AMERICA (national)	1998	8,000	1.3% in past 12 months 22.1% ever in any relationship	U.S. Department of Justice 1998
WEST BANK & GAZA STRIP (national; Palestinians)	1994	2,410	52.0% in past 12 months	Haj-Yahia 1998

Compiled by reference to the listed studies and *The World's Women 1990*, Statistics Canada Catalogue no. 85-224, p. 18; and "Population Reports," *Issues in World Health* 27, no. 4 (1999). See also <www.who.int/violence_injury_prevention/pages/who_prevalence_of_physical_viole.htm>.

in which they are currently involved, at least one in every five women (20 percent) in India, Kenya, Thailand and Uganda reports physical abuse. Finally, when the referent point is physical abuse at some point in her life, at least one in every five women (20 percent) in the following countries has been abused: Australia, Bangladesh, Canada, Chile, Egypt, Ethiopia, India, Kenya, Rwanda, South Africa, Thailand, Turkey, Uganda, United Kingdom, United States of America, and West Bank and Gaza Strip.

Studies may differ in their funding base, their research design, the exact wording of the questions, or how the research instruments are administered, but the overwhelming evidence of physical abuse of women worldwide cannot be ignored. Though the names of the researchers differ, as do their countries of origin and their training, the data gathered from the lives of ordinary women present consistent findings that women from every nation suffer physical violence at the hands of men with whom they have exchanged marriage vows or shared intimacy and residence.

The World's Women 1995, compiled by the United Nations Secretariat, has obtained internal studies from many additional countries. They report that the percentage of adult women who have been physically assaulted by an intimate partner exceeds one in three in Zam-

bia, the United Republic of Tanzania, Costa Rica, Ecuador, Guatemala, Japan, Suriname and Sri Lanka. The percentage falls between
25 and 30 percent in Antigua, Barbados and Belgium, and is 17 percent in New Zealand.

Sexual Violence

We turn from physical abuse and its impact on women to an examination of sexual violence. Table 2 presents data on the prevalence of sexual violence by intimate partners. "Sexual violence" refers to attempted
or completed sexual intercourse that is performed against a woman's
will. The proportion of women who report sexual violence range from
under one in ten in Canada (8 percent), Chile (9 percent), Puerto Rico
(6 percent) and the United States (8 percent) to rates well over one in
five in India (28 percent), Mexico (23-46 percent), Nicaragua (22 percent), Norway (17 percent), Peru (49 percent), Rwanda (33 percent),
Turkey (52 percent), United Kingdom (23 percent), West Bank and
Gaza Strip (38 percent), and Zimbabwe (25 percent).

Rape and Sexual Assault

While large-scale studies investigating rape and sexual assault are
rare, those that do exist reveal the high proportion of women and girls
who have experienced a rape or attempted rape at some point during
their lifetime.[15] Within both developed and developing nations around
the globe, rape and other forms of sexual assault are an ever-present
fear for scores of women, female children and teens. An article in the
World Health Statistics Quarterly in 1993 reported that statistics on sex
crimes include many victims aged ten or under.[16] Age data from
research in Peru, Malaysia, Mexico, Guatemala, Papua New Guinea
and Chile reveal that from 36 to 62 percent of sex crimes are perpetrated on victims aged fifteen or younger, and 13 to 32 percent involve
victims ten years old or younger. Comparable data from the United
States reveal that 62 percent of the victims of sex crimes are under the
age of sixteen and 29 percent have not yet reached eleven.

Although sexual assault may be committed by a stranger, in the
vast majority of cases the victim and the aggressor know one
another.[17] A sense of betrayal, then, is a central feature of the violence.

Table 2. Prevalence of Sexual Violence by Intimate Partners

Country (coverage area)	Year of study	Sample size	Percentage of adult women who have been sexually victimized by an intimate male partner	Publication information
CANADA (national)	1993	12,300	8.0% sexual assault in any relationship	Rodgers 1994; *Statistics Canada* 1993
CANADA (Toronto)	1991-1992	420	15.3% attempted or completed forced sex in any relationship	Randall et al. 1995
CHILE (Santiago)	1997	310	9.1 % attempted or completed forced sex in past 12 months	Morrison et al. 1997
INDIA (Uttar Pradesh)	1996	6,926[18]	28.0% completed forced sex ever in any relationship	Narayana 1996
MEXICO (Durango City)	1996	384	42.0% sexual assault in any relationship	Ramirez et al. 1996
MEXICO (Metropolitan Guadalajara)	1996	650	15.0% sexual assault in past 12 months 23.0% sexual assault in any relationship	Ramirez et al. 1996
NICARAGUA (León)	1993	360	21.7% attempted or completed forced sex in any relationship	Ellsberg 1997
NICARAGUA (Managua)	1997	378	17.7% attempted or completed forced sex in past 12 months	Morrison et al. 1997
NORWAY (Trondheim)	1989	111	17.1% attempted or completed forced sex in any relationship	Schei 1989
PERU (Metropolitan Lima)	1997	359	48.5% attempted or completed forced sex in past 12 months	Gonzales et al. 1997
PUERTO RICO (national)	1993-1996	7,079	5.7% completed forced sex in any relationship	Departamento de Salud y la Escuela 1998
RWANDA (Kigali)	1990	874	33.0% attempted or completed forced sex in past 12 months	Van der Straten et al. 1995

Country (coverage area)	Year of study	Sample size	Percentage of adult women who have been sexually victimized by an intimate male partner	Publication information
SWITZER-LAND (national)	1994-96	1,500	11.7% attempted or completed forced sex in any relationship	Gillioz et al. 1996
TURKEY (East and Southeast Anatolia)	1998	599	51.9% completed forced sex in any relationship	Ilkkaracan et al. 1998
UNITED KINGDOM (North London)	1993	430	6.0% attempted or completed forced sex in past 12 months 23.0% attempted or completed forced sex in any relationship	Mooney 1993
UNITED STATES OF AMERICA (national)	1995	8,000	0.2% attempted or completed forced sex in past 12 months 7.7% completed forced sex in any relationship	U.S. Department of Justice 1998
UNITED STATES OF AMERICA (Houston and S.E. Texas)	1991	300	14.7% attempted or completed forced sex in any relationship	McFarlane 1991
WEST BANK & GAZA STRIP (national; Palestinians)	1995	2,410	37.6% sexual assault in past 12 months 27.0% completed forced sex in past 12 months	Haj-Yahia 1998
ZIMBABWE (one province)	1996	885	25.0% attempted or completed forced sex in any relationship	Watts 1997

Compiled by reference to the listed studies and *The World's Women 1990*, Statistics Canada Catalogue no. 85-224, p. 18. See also <www.who.int/violence_injury_prevention/pages/who_prevalence_of_physical_viole.htm>.

When the sexual violence is perpetrated by a father, uncle, brother, grandfather or another adult male relative, the victim must sort out myriad feelings, ambiguities and contradictions. She may feel both love and hate. She may be dependent economically on the abuser or

fear reprisal should her tale of abuse be voiced. Other times the viola-
tor is not a family member but a trusted adult—a coach, teacher or
religious leader. Here too betrayal occurs: the sense of trust has been
broken, and the victim's vulnerability is marked.[19]

Moreover, thousands of women worldwide are coerced or otherwise abducted into forced prostitution or sold through other forms of
trafficking in women. Domestic workers and migrant women are
especially vulnerable to rape and violent attack by their employers,
who may withhold not only their wages but access to important personal documents and passports.

The desire to keep rape or sexual assault a secret is especially powerful in cultural contexts where a woman's virginity is a sign of personal and family honor, not to mention a prerequisite for marriage.
Since shame is attached to rape, the victim may wish to protect both
her future and the honor of her family.

In order to deal with the multitude of pressing problems that surface after sexual attack, many countries have set up rape crisis hot-
lines and rape crisis centers. In some jurisdictions there are special
rape crisis emergency rooms at local hospitals or uniquely trained
teams of women officers and healthcare workers who deal with victims of such trauma.

Violence against women and children is also a byproduct of armed
conflict and can include random acts of aggression—including sexual
violation—by both enemy and "friendly" forces; sometimes mass rape
is even a strategy of war.[20] Where there is displacement of large numbers of women and children as refugees, suffering can take the form of
the demand of sex for survival—a woman may be forced to exchange
sexual favors for food or shelter or the protection of her children.
Gang rape (more than one perpetrator per woman or girl child) and
forced pregnancy are also more common situations involving armed
conflict and military personnel. Sometimes women are seen as "territory" to be conquered or plundered; the violation of women and girl
children is meant to exacerbate men's humiliation and pain.

There are many forms of exploitation directed toward women and
girl children, including female genital mutilation (FGM)[21] and son
preference.[22] Victims of FGM are estimated at more than 130 million

individuals around the globe, with a further two million girls at risk of this practice.[23] In several areas of the world, boy children are more highly valued than girls. In extreme cases this may lead to violence against the girl child or female infanticide; less extreme cases can include less access to food, health care or education for girl children.

The Dynamics of Abuse

This section addresses some of the frequently asked questions related to violence against women and other forms of family violence. For those who have not experienced abuse themselves or witnessed it in their family of origin, it is often very hard to understand why abuse occurs, why victims do not leave abusive homes and why the cycle of violence is so often repeated in the next generation. While our treatment of these issues cannot possibly be exhaustive, we believe it is very important for Christians to become as informed as possible on abuse, its manifestations and its consequences.

> **Women in the United States are about six times more likely than men to experience violence committed by an intimate; women of all races are about equally vulnerable to abuse.** (Bureau of Justice Statistics, August 1995, based on U.S. Department of Justice, National Crime Victimization Survey, 1992-1993)

Why do so many men abuse their wives? Three main sources of data help researchers learn about abusive men: in-depth interviews with abused women who report on the behavior and personal characteristics of the men who battered them; regional or national surveys (like those reported in table 1) in which men self-identify their abusive behavior; and statements from those who are participating in programs for men who abuse their wives or girlfriends.

In their book *Behind Closed Doors*, Murray Straus, Richard Gelles and Susan Steinmetz argue that the greater the gap between the economic and prestige resources of a husband and a wife, the greater the man's tendency to maintain his dominant position in the marriage and the family by resorting to force.[24] As a result, abuse may follow a man's problems with work or periods of unemployment.[25] Abusive husbands are more likely to perceive their wives' behavior as threatening their sense of self, so men who have low self-esteem to begin with have a greater tendency to use force when they perceive their power challenged.[26] Other researchers claim that higher levels of general aggression in abusive men interact with certain features of their families of origin, like violence, poor communication skills and a lack of self-confidence.[27] Estimates suggest that between 50 and 75 percent of the men who batter their wives experienced or witnessed abuse in their own childhood home.[28] One family research laboratory has argued that young boys who have watched their father beat their mother have a 1,000 percent greater likelihood of violence in adulthood than boys who never undergo this painful childhood experience.[29] There is compelling evidence that violence is learned behavior, and most often it is learned in the home.[30]

> One in five women in Switzerland has experienced physical or sexual violence, and 40 percent have suffered from psychological violence by a husband or intimate partner. Women who are victims of such abuse are twice as likely as other women to be taking sedatives or tranquilizers.
> (Amnesty International 1995)

In a small-scale study conducted in the Boston area, James Ptacek explores how abusive men themselves understand and account for their violence.[31] Participants in a program for men who batter rationalized their violence through both excuses ("It was the booze") and justifications ("She bruises easily").[32] According to Ptacek's research, abusive men resort to violence to silence their partner or to punish her for failing to be the "perfect" wife.[33]

While there is evidence that some couples initiate violent acts equally,[34] in the majority of cases it is the man, not the woman, who controls whether there will be abuse in the home.[35] According to Larry Bennett, a professor of social work, many violent men claim that their wives can be violent at times too, but none of the violent men he has counseled have ever reported that they "were afraid to go home at night."[36]

The role of alcohol is often overestimated in explanations of why men batter. While many abusive husbands blame their battery on excessive drinking, actually the husbands who batter when drinking also batter when sober.[37] In fact, contrary to conventional wisdom, in more than 50 percent of abuse cases there is no consumption of alcoholic beverages at all.[38]

Why do women remain with partners who abuse them? Whether we are teaching in the university classroom, delivering a paper at a scholarly conference, offering a workshop for clergy or social service providers, speaking at a women's retreat or preaching in a Bible-centered church, people always ask why women stay in abusive relationships. Sometimes the question is asked in a public setting; sometimes it is voiced in private. Those who have never experienced violence personally find it hard to understand the ties that make it difficult for women to extricate themselves from an abusive environment. On the other hand, the question on the minds of those who have direct experience is voiced like this: "How can a woman ever muster the courage to actually leave?" Thus personal experience of abuse frames one's understanding dramatically.

For any individual woman, of course, the reason it is difficult to terminate a violent relationship (temporarily or forever) is complex. In just a few paragraphs it is impossible to cover all the reasons staying put seems more beneficial than leaving. We are not necessarily advocating that all women must or should leave an abusive marriage permanently, but we would *never* suggest that a woman *ought* to remain in a context that puts her life at risk or threatens the safety of her children. But why is leaving even on a temporary basis such a difficult decision?

Fear is the number-one reason women do not leave abusive husbands and violent homes.[39] A battered wife fears for her future, fears further violence and fears for the lives of her children. In fact, fear permeates her life and is often experienced as a paralyzing terror, ruling her day and destroying her sleep through nightmares. Fear makes women lie about the reality of the abuse ("the bruise on my face is because I fell down the basement stairs"). And fear hampers women's ability to see the choices they might make to enhance their personal safety. So they spend what energy they have left trying to keep the secret rather than trying to escape.

Finances—economic dependency—keep many women from perceiving that there are any options to life without their violent husband. Many abusive men are good providers of the food, housing and clothing their wives and children need. A woman's lack of personal or economic resources, coupled with the fact that she might never have been employed in the labor market, means she cannot see any alternatives. How would she provide for her children without money or a job? How could she obtain employment if her skills have been used primarily at home since the children were born? Where could she flee and who would offer her refuge? Thus some battered women believe that the violence they experience is their "payment" for food, housing and their children's schooling. Added to this, many abused women feel so poorly about themselves that they actually consider that they deserve their husbands' battering. Family violence researchers have argued that a woman's level of economic dependence on her husband is a major factor in whether she will remain in an abusive environment, or return to a violent husband after a temporary respite.[40]

Fantasy of change, or the hope that someday the violence will cease, keeps many women with violent husbands for years or for a lifetime.[41] After abuse there may be remorse. After the violence there may be pleas for forgiveness. After the pain there may be promises of change. Although the evidence suggests that few batterers do alter their abusive ways,[42] many women cling to that hope, that fantasy, year after year. Religious women are especially likely to cling to the belief that their violent husband wants to and will change his violent behavior.[43]

As Nancy has argued in *The Battered Wife: How Christians Confront Family Violence*, religious batterers often manipulate pastors and other Christian people by employing religious words, including Scripture, to ensure that there is reunion between their wives and themselves, the violated and the violent.[44] The minister with little counseling experience or training in responding to abuse may find it difficult to distinguish between the inauthentic plea of a manipulative man and the genuine repentance of a husband sorry for the violence of his past and committed to altering his abusive ways.

In essence, women remain with the men who abuse them because they are fearful, because they lack the economic or social resources to leave, and because they cling tightly to the hope that someday he will change. In addition, some religious women feel that God does not permit them to leave, that marriage is forever no matter how cruel their

> It is estimated that twenty-five thousand women are victims of rape each year in Peru; the majority of these women have not yet reached fourteen years of age.
> (<www.igc.org/iwraw/publications/countries/peru.html>)

husband's treatment, that this may be their cross to bear, or that perpetual forgiveness of their husband for his repeated behavior is God's expectation. For women such as these, it is often very difficult to sort out the difference between long-suffering in honor to Christ and to their marriage vows and actively contributing to the danger of their own lives. The wise pastor will help such a woman navigate these troubled waters.

Consequences of Woman Abuse

Violence against women exacts an enormous cost, especially for the victim and her children. Often not considered, though, are health care costs, judicial costs and the effects on productivity and employment. For the victim, there are immediate and longer-term physical consequences. Most dramatic in this regard are homicide statistics. Numerous studies worldwide examine deaths caused by the violence of an intimate partner. In a study of 249 court records in Zimbabwe it was found that 59 percent of female homicides were committed by an intimate partner of the victim.[45] Where arranged marriages and dowry practices exist, women who are unable to meet the demands for gifts or money sometimes sacrifice their own lives through suicide, or die at the hands of a husband or his family.

Women sustain a variety of injuries as a result of violence perpetrated against them. In Papua New Guinea, for example, 18 percent of all married women sought emergency-room treatment in the aftermath of domestic violence. In Cambodia[46] it was found that 50 percent of all women who disclosed that they had been the victim of wife abuse sustained physical injuries, while in Canada the figure was 45 percent.[47]

A study of 1,203 pregnant women in the American cities of Houston and Boston found that violence toward a mother during pregnancy was a significant risk factor for low birth weight of her child.[48] Moreover, unwanted and early pregnancies are sometimes the result of rape, as are sexually transmitted diseases such as HIV/AIDS.

There is also growing evidence of the longer-term psychological consequences of violence, such as suicide attempts, mental and emotional health problems, and the effects on children of witnessing violence against their mother. When other factors are held constant, abused women are six times more likely to experience emotional and psychological distress than nonabused women.[49] Children who watch the victimization of their mothers are five times more likely to exhibit serious behavioral problems than other children.[50]

2

Beginning
to Respond

We hope that after reading the statistics and the stories, you are asking yourself some questions: What can one person do? Might I be able to reach out to someone in my community or church? Or the question might be framed in a broader context. What can one congregation do? Could I raise this issue at a board meeting, or discuss it with my pastor, or alert my Bible study group to the prevalence of violence in the home? Could my congregation catch a vision of supporting victims of violence and condemning abusive acts in our community? Or the issue could be framed from a global perspective: What would happen if evangelical churches around the world joined in condemning violence and supporting its victims?

World Health Assembly Resolution 49.25 proclaims violence to be a public health issue. It calls for concerted action by health care workers around the globe and commits the WHO to the publication of guidelines and standards to address this most urgent issue.

We think that alliances of churches around the globe need to consider violence against women a religious issue, an issue demanding thoughtful and immediate response from denominations and ministry organizations right down to the grass-roots level—the local congregation.

Hearing the Voices

While a global perspective is important—indeed imperative—for giving us a vision of the need of victims and the immense problem of violence against women, individual acts of kindness and support usually begin on home territory. Here we present some voices—of victims, of caregivers and of clergy—that paint a picture of what congregations can accomplish when hearts are stirred by the suffering of women around the world and in their own backyard.

Voices of Victims

But when I became a Christian, I was thankful to the Lord because I had a pastor who . . . knew what I'd been through, and he didn't judge me. And he was the type of pastor who was working with women who had been through . . . abusive marriages.[1]

I spent 15 years in a violent home with my first husband and I think that at one point I wouldn't have wanted interference, but then again if I had a sense that it was there, I might have been able to get help.[2]

Voices of Women Helping Women

Cheryl was a young woman—not yet thirty—who lived in a coastal community. She bore the scars of repeated episodes of abuse from her common-law husband, a large-framed, ex-military man. Although Cheryl herself did not belong to any particular community of believers, her relationship with the local evangelical church was mediated by a faithful member, a neighbor, named Sue. Cognizant of Cheryl's fear, and her husband's intimidating ways, Susan helped to organize a move to a safe new location. One Saturday morning, with Cheryl's husband occupied at his job, Sue's team of volunteers packed up Cheryl's belongings and transported them to a new apartment, miles away in another town. Sue's husband drove his pick-up truck and several church members helped to load the furniture and other items belonging to Cheryl. As Sue shared this story, she emphasized how impossible it would have been for Cheryl to have been able to escape the abusive environment without the support of men and women of faith.[3]

Voices of Clergy
I thank the Lord that I'm a great big two-hundred pound guy because . . . I've had a husband who was violent against his wife haul off and hit me and all I could think about was these glasses cost me two hundred dollars and I don't want to get them broken. . . . I see the violence against women and it makes me mad, and there's a lot of it going on.[4]

Choosing the path of least resistance. That's probably her way of contributing to the conflict in that [violent] relationship . . . by staying.[5]

Strategic Thinking
How might the evangelical church—its leaders and its people—help bridge the chasm between the pain of victims and the hope of the gospel? Appropriate response to an individual can never be determined in advance of hearing the pain she has endured and the practical help she seeks. Yet we will suggest some basic ground-rules that may enable congregations and individuals to augment the healing journey of victims.

It is very important to hold offenders accountable for both their past abusive behavior and their promise of changed actions. Ultimately, all believers need to promote violence-free family living by modeling appropriate and healthy reactions to disappointment and disagreement. The role of church leaders and church programs in teaching, encouraging and mentoring such behavior is vital and should never be underestimated.

Congregations and church leaders need to begin a soul-searching process related to violence against women and other forms of family violence. While change is always difficult, the gospel tells us that we do not need to be the same people we were in the past, that the old person and the old ways can be altered by God's transforming power, that with new insight, powered by God's Holy Spirit, our actions tomorrow can be more in keeping with the life and compassion of Christ than our behavior was yesterday. This message rings true at both the individual and corporate levels. Sometimes we need to acknowledge our individual mistakes and repent. Sometimes as congregations we need to acknowledge our failings and repent. Sometimes as organizations we need to admit our shortcomings and repent. In order to respond with the mind of Christ to the suffering of abuse victims worldwide, we will need to search our individual, congregational and organizational souls. This process will be painful, but without it change is impossible.

> The Norwegian Health Authorities have estimated that each year approximately ten thousand women contact a hospital in Norway because of family violence.
> (<www.wave-network.org/articles/429.htm>)

There are many men and women around the globe who have never been violent toward a partner or a child. We rejoice in that fact. But often these same people have never felt compassion toward victims of violence because they have no eyes to see their suffering or ears to hear their cries. This book aims to address that lack. We believe that once people of faith and church leaders have been confronted with the wrenching reality of the prevalence of violence, they will want to do something about it.

Rhetoric Versus Reality

Martha and her husband, Daniel, were key laypeople in First Presbyterian Church of Birch Grove, a picturesque bedroom community to which large numbers of men and women retreat after a long working day in the nearby industrial city. She worked in the denominational headquarters as an office manager, and he held the elected position of Sunday School superintendent in their local church. Together they sang in the choir, and their home served as a comfortable location for many church executive meetings. They were any pastor's dream couple—attractive, talented, relatively affluent, hardworking people who wanted to contribute to the weekly routine of church life. But Martha and Daniel had a secret: he was an abusive husband and she was a battered wife.

The abuse started when Martha was three months pregnant with their first child. They had gone out for a social evening at a friend's home. In the car on the way home Daniel accused Martha of talking to some of the men at the party. Caught by surprise, Martha retorted that they were longtime friends of all of these couples and that during the course of the evening she had talked to everyone who was present. When they got home, he called her a whore and hit her across the face.

Martha and Daniel lived the lie for years; eventually they had four young children and resided in a large, two-story house in an enviable neighborhood, but Martha's salary alone could not support food, rent for an apartment, and the children's music and sports activities, let alone money for church projects. She felt trapped, alone and afraid.

Sometimes life was good and Martha was lulled into believing that Daniel had changed. He was often repentant after an abusive episode, and in the early years of their marriage she clung to the hope that someday he would be less abusive and that she would be a better wife. Years passed and the children entered high school. Then an incident occurred that caused Martha to call the police, fearing that Daniel was going to kill her.

They had gone several weeks without speaking to each other, and she broke the silence one evening as she stood at the sink, he at the stove, both preparing the supper meal. Her voice and her words about the vegetables threw him into a rage. Daniel grabbed her and started pounding her head into the kitchen cupboard, making an effort not to bruise her face so as to call forth the sympathy of others. As Martha told me her story, tears streamed down her face, but then she smiled a little. "My head made so much noise banging those cupboards that Carla, our teenage daughter, came downstairs." Once Carla entered the kitchen, the banging stopped.

It was difficult for Martha to recount exactly what happened in the aftermath of this violent outburst. But the police were called, an arrest was made, and Daniel was escorted temporarily from their home. To her astonishment, the clergyman for whom she worked did not believe her story, despite the fact that Daniel was in jail for the weekend. In a nutshell, Daniel was simply too nice a man—a fine Christian man at that—to ever harm anyone, especially his wife. Martha disclosed the story to no one else.

Her life was now surrounded by a new lie: she and Daniel had irreconcilable differences and they were going to seek a divorce. Her denominational employer was fearful of what people might think about a divorced woman as office manager; her local pastor was fearful of what congregants might think about a divorced Sunday school superintendent. No one seemed to be fearful for the safety of Martha and her children.

The healing process was slow, much slower than Martha had hoped. While the children were supportive, even they did not understand the full extent of Martha's pain or its long history. It was too difficult to tell them; in fact, she wanted them to harbor predominantly pleasant childhood memories, memories where the abuse was still hidden. It was important to Martha that they remember their childhood as one characterized by the words *happy Christian family*. For Martha, though, such a family existed only in her dreams.[6]

Evangelicals feel very passionate about the family and speak warmly and enthusiastically about the importance of "family values." In many parts of the world, religious people are deeply committed to particular notions of the family and often bemoan the fact that the

> A fifty-year-old man from Kenya beat his wife to death with a stool after she allegedly failed to serve him dinner on time. She was late returning home after selling vegetables at the market. (*Kenya Times*, August 4, 1999)

family is under attack by secular forces in contemporary culture. With the Scripture close at hand, evangelicals teach that God planned for men and women to choose lifelong partners and to share the joys and burdens of parenthood until death drew their work to a close. Socializing the young, teaching them spiritual truths and offering them a skill and knowledge base from which to live their lives is at the core of what Christians claim to be doing in a family setting.

The mechanics of how this is accomplished, though, differ according to the surrounding culture and one's social location within it. Time also has an impact, for our culture and its norms are ever-changing. Though God is not limited by time, how we humans express our love and devotion to others and what skills and knowledge we believe are essential for our children differ according to the place and age in which we live. Understandings of the family do not remain static, they are ever-changing, adapting both to the increasing information available to us and our response to it.

Christians need to realize that while passion for family living and family values may feel timeless, how that is communicated and carried out in any place or any given generation will differ. We must be on our guard to ensure that nostalgia for the traditional family, however that is defined, does not prevent us from ministering to the real needs of our communities. In fact, one person's nostalgia may be another person's nightmare: the white picket fence, the 2.5 kids, the dog and the family van are not universal nor particularly sacred. They are laden with cultural and class values, not necessary godless in themselves, but not necessarily emanating from the heart of God. In other words, the image is not meaningful for everyone, nor does it produce warm fuzzies for all.

How do these nostalgic images and evangelical musings on the traditional family link to violence? you may wonder. The answer is quite straightforward. We teach and preach that the family is sacred, ordained by God, honored by Christian people. The family may be sacred, but sometimes it is not safe.[7] In our enthusiasm to support the family, we often overlook that important fact. Statistically speaking, women, men and children are more likely to be harmed or threatened or injured within their own family home than outside it. When we place the family on a very high pedestal, we must recognize that the result is a chasm between those whose experience of family life—in their childhood or adult life—differs dramatically from the picture we paint in our Sunday-morning sermons or teach through the Sunday-school curriculum.

We must recognize the reality of families in crisis and in pain. There are many women and children who arrive in our churches on Sunday and return home to an environment where their physical and mental health cannot be assured. For those of us who claim the family as a central building block in our nations and our churches, it is essential to take responsibility for responding to families in crisis. The rhetoric may draw on images of happy family living. But the real experience of many men, women and children is very different. Taken too far, the notion of "happy family living" blinds people to the plight of those who suffer in the family context. Taken too far, "happy family living" excuses some family members from living and acting as responsible, caring people. Taken too far, the family becomes a battle zone where the rules of culture do not apply.

While ensuring healthy and safe family living should appeal to all humans everywhere, it should be especially crucial for those of us who claim the label *Christian*. We preach and teach that the family is very important to God. But we often act otherwise. Does our church programming take into account that many women, men and children do not live in an intact nuclear family? Do we have support and assistance for families in crisis? How do we teach our families to cope with disappointment and anger?

> During 1997, 1,030 women and 1,065 children were admitted to one of sixteen shelters in Austria for which data was available; 237 endangered women had to be turned away. (<www.wave-network.org/articles/111.htm>)

Where can families connected to our faith communities turn when they need resources or counsel? What happens when an abused woman looks for help in your church?

We say we believe in the family, but sometimes our programming suggests that it is only certain kinds of families we hold dear. We say it is important for children to grow up in a loving environment, but do we offer assistance to mothers and fathers who are in turmoil? We say that family happiness is a gift from God, but can women who fear for their lives at the hands of their violent husbands find support and respite in our congregations?

What are some ways that churches around the world might respond to the level and severity of violence against women evidenced in tables 1 and 2? There are both healthy and unhealthy options.

Unhealthy Responses

Lack of Awareness

☐ If wife abuse was really that common, I would have heard much more talk about it before.

☐ It might be occurring in other parts of the world, but it is not happening much in my local area and certainly not in my church.

☐ I can't think of a single man who would raise his fist against his wife.

☐ Some people deserve the terrible things that happen to them.

☐ I wonder what women do to make their husbands that mad at them.

☐ I have never heard my pastor talk about it, so it can't be a problem in my church.

Resistance to Condemnation

☐ What happens in someone else's family is none of my business.

☐ If it was that bad, she would just leave.

☐ How can I condemn abuse when I don't understand all the circumstances?

☐ There's nothing I can do to stop another person's abuse.

☐ Talking about these issues may make matters worse.

Lack of Education

☐ No one will come to my Bible study again if I raise the issue of violence.

☐ I am not going to talk about it; it makes me feel uncomfortable.

☐ Men do not like to hear the pastor say things like this.

☐ It would embarrass people in the congregation.

Lack of Prevention

☐ If it is going to happen, there is nothing anyone can do about it.

☐ Some people are born to be violent, and there is no way to help them.

☐ Talking about violence will turn people away from the church.

Lack of Empathy

☐ I could never help anyone who is a victim of violence.

☐ I don't want to know if someone in my church acts this way.

☐ People should keep their troubles to themselves.

☐ I have enough of my own problems, I don't want to know about the problems of others.

☐ I might say the wrong thing if I were to try to help someone.

Lack of Referrals

☐ The church has no business helping in the community.

☐ Some of the agencies in the community are very negative about the church, so we should keep to ourselves.

☐ Women who are abused do not need legal help or social assistance.

☐ Violence within church families must be hidden from the community where churches are built.

Such responses don't work and don't bring credit to the cause of Christ. We must find our way to much healthier responses, discover ways that churches around the world can respond to the suffering created by violence against women.

Healthy Responses

Awareness

☐ Be committed to increasing the awareness of pastors and church people about abuse.

☐ Recognize that family violence and wife abuse exist in every nation around the world.

☐ Help congregations see that violence exists among church families as well as families living in the neighborhoods where churches are located.

☐ Use posters and information packets to alert church attenders to the seriousness of violence in the home.

☐ Offer training materials to pastors and lay workers in local church settings.

☐ Use illustrations in sermons and other teaching materials that make it safe for someone to come forward to disclose violence in her own life.

Condemnation of Abusive Behavior

☐ Speak out about abusive behavior whenever an opportunity presents itself.

☐ Let governments and nongovernmental agencies alike know that the church stands firm in its opposition to spouse abuse and violence in the home.

☐ Make it clear to church people that God does not condone men's battering women or women's battering men.

☐ Whenever possible, ensure that Christians and the church are counted among those opposed to wife battering or any form of family violence.

Education

☐ Make sure that Bible colleges, seminaries and other training centers for pastors include in their curriculum information on spouse abuse and family violence.

☐ In Sunday-school teaching and in Bible studies, emphasize how important it is for men and women to deal with their frustrations and disappointments in nonviolent ways.

> The World Health Organization says that one in five women around the globe is physically or sexually abused in her lifetime.

☐ When pastors meet with couples seeking to get married, emphasize resolving conflict without abuse.

☐ In training teachers and other nonordained workers in the church, alert them to the prevalence of violence and offer them help in responding to victims.

Prevention

☐ Model loving, nonabusive behavior in the families of pastors and other church leaders.

☐ Be explicit in helping families know where they can turn for help.

☐ In youth activities, encourage young men and women to treat each other well and to respect each other's abilities and points of view.

☐ Help newly married couples to resolve differences and seek help when necessary.

Empathy

☐ Help men and women learn to listen to each other and be interested in the lives of other people in the church and in the community.

☐ Offer safe places to talk about life's disappointments and problems (e.g., small group fellowship, women's Bible study, men's prayer breakfast).

☐ When you promise someone confidentiality, ensure you mean it and keep your promise.

☐ Practice acts of kindness that help others know you care about them.

☐ Learn to rejoice with those who are happy and to weep with those who are sad.

Referrals

☐ Be aware of the resources in your area to help hurting families.

☐ Know the name of the local shelter for battered women and how to access help there.

☐ Volunteer church resources to assist community initiatives dealing with wife abuse.

☐ Think about what particular gifts and ministries the church has to offer victims of family violence.

☐ Publicize the church's mission to abuse victims in local shelters or other community agencies.

This list of healthy responses to problems of violence is simply meant to get Christians thinking about all the ways pastors and their people can encourage and model healthy living, and provide resources and help to those who suffer from violence. Later we will provide a more in-depth discussion of strategies for responding to abuse; for now it is important to realize that only as we become aware of the nature and extent of the suffering of women, children and families can we be motivated to do something about it.

To this point we have only hinted at the Christian call to compassion and the scriptural injunction to rescue those who live in fear. Having established the reality of violence against women in our world, we turn to God's Word for guidance, instruction and comfort. *Hear the Word of the Lord!*

3

Growing in
Compassion

C arol and Joe struggled just to survive. There was never enough money to pay the bills, never permanent employment, never marital harmony. Moreover, Joe tended to drink excessively. And there were school problems with the oldest child, a boy who had been diagnosed with ADD (attention deficit disorder). Always Carol and Joe feared that the future would be worse than the present. Because money was scarce, there were few family outings, few unexpected treats for the children and very few evenings or weekends of fun. To be sure, Carol and her children had happy moments, when her mother would invite them to the country and the children could run free, or times when Joe would be called in to do mechanic work on the weekend and the extra money would enable him to take the son to McDonald's and bowling, allowing Carol and the girls a break from all that noise and activity. And there were times when all five of them would go to the park on a Sunday afternoon. But for the most part Carol and Joe did not enjoy each other's company, and they found the children burdensome.

Carol's father had been abusive toward her mother and one of her brothers. Joe himself had been a victim of child abuse; as a man he bore the physical and emotional scars of poverty and violence. Both Carol and Joe suffered from low self-esteem and a sense of hopelessness and powerlessness. Joe had "done time" in a local jail and "time in a rooming house," when he had been given a court order to live apart from Carol.

At the time I became aware of Carol and Joe's story, a particular church community had taken them under its wing. Carol was participating in a young mothers' group, Joe was receiving individual counsel from the pastor, Carol was offered the services of a Christian counselor (paid for by church sources), and the children had been integrated into age-appropriate programs in the church; moreover, church women were supporting the family through ongoing contact and acts of kindness, such as childcare and gifts of clothing and food. According to Carol, Joe had been nonabusive for over a year, and she was working part time at a garden center. Life was far from easy, but it was looking much better than it ever had in the past.

> In 1998 a woman was set ablaze in Vanasthalipuram, India, after she refused to seek more dowry from her father. She was doused with kerosene and set on fire, and consequently died. (*The Hindu*, July 26, 1998)

The violence was condemned, the fear was acknowledged, and the couple were offered choices. According to Carol, most of her church contacts (including the pastoral staff) had encouraged her to leave Joe and begin a new life free from the violence of the past.

But because she was reluctant to do that, the faith community was working to help the family reach the goal of abuse-free family living. The support had been ongoing for over two years at the time I first met Carol. By her own account, church women took her places, brought groceries, and came and looked after the children while she was at work, and the missionary group had raised money for her at Christmas. One woman had taken her on a weeklong vacation, and another sister in the faith had cared for the children.

While the story offers no dramatic turnaround or quick solution to the social and economic difficulties Carol and Joe faced, it is clearly an example of support for an abused woman and her children—and the perpetrator of that violence as well—within a church congregation. And if change is to occur within Carol's family, that support from the faith community will need to continue for a very long time![1]

Called to Compassion
"Who is my neighbor?" a teacher of the law asked Jesus. In response Jesus told the parable of the good Samaritan. "And who was the neighbor?" Jesus asked in return. The answer was painfully obvious: the one who saw the need, bandaged the wounds, transported the traveler and paid for extended care and lodging.

Our social action, or response to what we see around us, derives its motivation and vision from the practical ministry of our leader, Jesus of Nazareth. Let us consider three examples of Christ's earthly ministry which we might wish to imitate as we respond to victims of abuse and violence.

Jesus nourished the crowds by offering them both spiritual and physical food. By particular acts of kindness on our lifelong journey of compassion, we earn the respect of others and the right to witness to God's love in our hearts and lives. Throughout Jesus' travels with his disciples and the women among the entourage, Jesus showed concern for the physical well-being of his followers; when they were hungry, Jesus fed them; when they were weary, he offered them rest; and when the disciples were frightened, he calmed the seas.

Jesus washed the disciples' feet. As the heart of our Lord was being prepared for his own imminent suffering, Jesus planned one last meal for the disciples to have together. And he welcomed each one by washing their feet. What an interesting model for us! Even when his betrayal and death were close at hand, Jesus ministered to those more needy than himself. Can we put aside our own needs and desires long enough to see the needs of others? Where and with whom do we have washing that needs to be done?

Jesus wept over the death of Lazarus. Jesus' compassion for those around him was remarkable. Not only did he realize their need, but he took on their pain. Why did Jesus weep over Lazarus, when he knew that life could be breathed into that dead body? Because Jesus cared for him—because he loved him and was emotionally involved with this man and his two sisters, Mary and Martha. Jesus wept over Lazarus not because of his death but because of the pain and sadness that it created. When we love people, we too will weep for them, even as we know that their circumstances can be altered and that we can play a role in that transformation.

When we imitate the life of Christ, we will be involved in feeding, washing and weeping. How? First, by validating the pain of someone who is hurting. Studies conducted by the Religion and Violence Research Team in Canada have revealed that one of the most helpful ways women of faith have assisted abused women has been through the offer of a listening ear: "Taking children, being a listening ear, a grocery person, taxi driver. Just seeing a need and doing it before they have to ask, just to make . . . life easier."[2]

When we listen to others' stories, we validate their experience. Our silence and our attention says, *What has happened to you is important to me: I am willing to listen.* We can tell people until the cows come home that we are interested in them, but if we never listen intently to what they have to say, our words are like a tinkling bell or a clanging cymbal (1 Cor 13:1).

> Female genital mutilation, or female circumcision, is practiced in as many as twenty-eight African countries and in a couple of countries outside of Africa.
> (<www.jhuccp.org/pr/j45/j45chap3_3.stm>)

Listening to a person's story is not the same thing as evaluating it or judging its accuracy—that is the responsibility of legally trained professionals and the justice system. People in pain report that the first step toward healing and recovery is simply to have someone to hear them out, someone who is empathic and sensitive, slow to speak and eager to listen. While listening can be hard work, it really doesn't take any special training or advanced skills. A good listener shows interest in the person and what information they are sharing. It's speaking and advice-giving that require advanced education and wisdom.

The Christian call to compassion is first and foremost a call to meet people where they are, to see the reality of their plight, to hear the cry of their heart and attempt to understand their pain. Somewhere in the healing journey it may be necessary for someone with professional training to sort through all the dynamics of their past and their present, and to evaluate the accuracy of their story, the long-term impact of what they have suffered, and all the precipitating factors. Though such a process is important, the first need of abuse victims is for someone to listen, empathize and assist them in locating the practical and emotional help that they need to continue living.

Mending Broken Hearts

Bonnie suffered tremendous verbal and sexual abuse from her husband James, a man who was successful in business but preoccupied most of his waking hours with matters of sex. He dreamed of being a pimp, someone who could fulfill his own sexual fantasies at the same time that he was coordinating the sexual activities of several young women.

Jim wanted Bonnie to dress provocatively to seduce any man she met at church or in the community. He insisted that she dress without underwear; to accomplish this unreasonable request, he would often take her undergarments and hide them. For five years she endured constant discussion of her body and daily behavior that made her uncomfortable in private and in public. During the latter phase of her life with Jim, his goal was to transform her into a prostitute.

Since Bonnie and Jim were evangelical Christians and attended a nondenominational church known for its active discipleship, she sought help and guidance from the leaders Despite her frequent pleas for assistance, no one was willing to take seriously her sexual abuse or challenge her husband on his behavior. From time to time she was encouraged to be loyal to him, but never to seek refuge or respite from the badgering she was forced to endure.

As a childhood victim of physical abuse and molestation, Bonnie was well acquainted with the survivor role. Consequently, it took her many years and the ongoing support of a Christian therapist to finally extricate herself from such an unhealthy environment. Describing the marriage as the worst chapter of her life, she confided that even now, many years later, the sexual abuse still torments her. Her broken heart is still in need of ongoing repair.[3]

*   *   *

The most basic form of Christian service is love in action—mending broken hearts. Christians will be identified by their love for one another (Jn 13:35). The task of mending suggests repair, fixing things that are broken. Isaiah 61 speaks of binding up the brokenhearted, comforting those who mourn, replacing mourning with gladness, offering a garment of praise in place of a spirit of despair. And how will this be accomplished? When God's people go up to Gilead and apply its healing balm to the wounds of those who suffer (cf. Jer 8:20-22; 46:11).

God has a passion for mending brokenness. Scripture is filled with passages in which the God of the universe shows compassion for the weak of this earth, like a hen that gathers her chicks under her wings (Mt 23:37). This is the picture of the Christian God: a deity who has the hairs of our head numbered, who cares about the feeding patterns of sparrows and the enduring beauty of lilies in a grassy meadow (Lk 7:24; 12:7, 27-28). How much more valuable, sister in Christ, brother in Christ, are you? How much more valuable indeed!

While there can be little doubt of God's interest in the heart-mending business, individuals must recognize their need of repair and congregations must be prepared to assist in the tasks of mending. God's mending does not occur in a factory, where hundreds of machines and machine operators sew clothing in a standard fashion. God's mending occurs one heart at a time—sometimes at the altar, sometimes at the kitchen table, sometimes during a walk in the woods, sometimes prompted by the words of another woman of faith, always prompted by the still small voice (1 Kings 19:11).

As people of faith we need to learn to recognize brokenness in ourselves and in those around us. We have to acknowledge our need to have the healing balm of Gilead applied to our afflictions, physical or emotional or spiritual. The God we serve, who loved us before we could love in return, is in the business of mending hearts, shattered dreams and broken bodies. To put it in the language of the day: the market niche of God's Spirit is heart repair. But how is the healing balm of Gilead applied? That's where you and I come in. That is the role of congregational life.

God chooses earthly vessels, jars of clay, ordinary people to assist in responding to the brokenness around us. There are many models of menders offered in Scripture: think of Dorcas, Phoebe, Priscilla or the unnamed stretcher bearers, each a conduit to the healing touch of Jesus.

The story of Dorcas is recorded in Acts 9. A woman named Tabitha, translated as Dorcas, lived in Joppa. She was constantly doing good and helping the poor and needy, especially widows. She would use a needle and thread in her upstairs room to sew garments for poor women who had nothing to wear. Clothing needy widows was her market niche. But she fell ill and died, and the church in Joppa begged Peter to redirect his travels in order that he could visit their town and touch her body. Somehow the Christian community in Joppa was convinced that its ministry opportunities would be thwarted without the talents and gifts of this old woman. Peter came. The church widows showed him the handmade garments Dorcas had crafted. Peter prayed. Dorcas arose.

> More than one million children—mostly female—are forced into prostitution each year, the majority in Asia. (<www.unicef.org/pon97/women1.htm>)

In the tradition of Dorcas, some today use domestic talents in service of Christ. This woman used some rather unsophisticated tools—a needle, some thread, a pair of scissors—to offer hope to needy women. Her ministry of clothing worked to mend some of the rips and tears that years of living had created. She was a sister of mercy before the name was adopted by Catholic nuns. And congregations can become sisters of mercy to families in crisis.

Phoebe's service to God and to the growing Christian community is recorded in Romans 16. Paul commends to his readers this woman, whom he calls a servant (or a deacon) of the church in Cenchreae, asking that they receive her in a manner worthy of the saints, offering her help and remembering her labor. How exactly did Phoebe serve the church? Among other tasks, female deacons in the early church prepared women candidates for baptism[4] and visited women and girls in their homes—which was not always appropriate for men to do. While

Dorcas was stitching broken hearts, Phoebe was washing them.

When the Christian church sets about bathing our lives, we do not feel dirty or shameful any longer. The old nature, replete with heartache and pain, is replaced with a new nature fashioned in likeness to Christ. The past is washed away. God's Spirit beckons us to start over—to mourn no longer, to rise and go forth, to put our hand to the plow and not look back.

While Dorcas stitches and Phoebe cleanses, Priscilla offers wise counsel. A tentmaker by trade, Priscilla and her husband Aquila began a house ministry in Ephesus, after being commissioned by Paul to leave their homestead in Corinth for the sake of ministry. Their family story, recorded in Acts 18, suggests that Priscilla used her talents both inside and outside the home to share the gospel and to reason in the synagogues—and often as she and Aquila sold their goods in the marketplace. She used her intellectual prowess to convince others of the efficacy of the gospel of Christ. She offered hope to the hopeless by words of wisdom, reason and truth.

The unnamed stretcher bearers who bring their friend to Jesus in Mark 2 are also ministers of healing balm. Four buddies had a paralyzed friend, and since they were unable to offer direct assistance for his malaise, they decided to bring him to the Jewish rabbi known for healing powers. When the friends carried him on a stretcher to the house where Jesus was staying, they found it so crowded that it was impossible to make their way inside. Undeterred by the obstacle of overcrowding, they climbed onto the roof, dug through it, and then lowered their friend into a room where Jesus was teaching.

It is a very interesting story of acknowledged human limitations and the power of spiritual strength, of perseverance in the face of obstacles, of what happens when people pool their resources to help someone in need. If our congregations were filled with friends like these—undeterred by obstacles because they were convinced of the necessity to get close to Jesus—imagine how many could be touched by the healing balm of Gilead.

Spiritual Shepherd
Pastor John ministers in an evangelical church of about 250 people in

eastern Canada. Like most clergy in the region, he is sometimes called on to intervene in homes that are riddled with conflict. "I've had a lady who has come to me out of fear for her own life and her children's lives, with a husband who . . . has come from an abusive home." This couple, Ruth and Sam, had been married for about eighteen years; almost from the beginning it was an unhappy relationship. "He has pushed and shoved her from time to time. But his scare tactic is to take his hunting rifle out and lay it on the bed and say, 'OK, I'm gonna shoot myself, I'm gonna shoot myself and somebody else.'" Ruth has endured this for years. She seeks out her pastor when things get really volatile. Her husband says he is sorry after a violent episode. According to the pastor, "he always comes back, in tears himself, remorseful and says he'll never do it again . . . only to repeat it." Both Pastor John and Ruth feel there is little hope for the marriage.[5]

As table 3 reveals, clergy are not strangers to family violence. A large proportion of ministers are called on to respond to women, men and children whose lives have been affected by violence within the family.

Table 3. Percentage of Canadian Clergy Who Have *Ever* Counseled in These Situations Involving Violence[6]

° A woman who has an abusive husband or partner	83.2
° A woman who was abused in childhood by a parent	77.2
° A couple whose relationship is often violent	74.0
° A man who is abusive toward his wife or partner	70.4
° A child/youth who has been abused by his/her father	67.7
° A father who is abusive of his children	57.0
° A man who was abused in childhood by a parent	53.3
° A woman whose husband is abusing the children	49.7
° A child/youth who has been abused by his or her mother	47.7
° A mother who is abusive of her children	46.3
° A teenager who has an abusive boyfriend	44.1
° A woman who is planning to marry an abusive boyfriend	43.6
° A man who has an abusive wife/partner	39.8
° A woman who is abusive toward her husband/partner	38.3
° A woman who is being abused by her son/daughter	30.9
° A man who is planning to marry an abusive girlfriend	12.5

For the purposes of our discussion, let's consider the data related to woman abuse and the most common such counseling situation for pastors: a woman with an abusive partner. Table 3 reveals that 83.2 percent of Canadian pastors report that during their ministry they have been called on to intervene in a situation involving a victimized woman and an abusive man, most often her legal husband. Looking more closely at the data, we observe that approximately *10 percent of Canadian clergy report that they respond to at least five battered women each year*, with the majority of pastors having regular, but less frequent, experiences of counseling battered wives. And their experience is not with abused women alone. Seventy percent of Canadian clergy claimed to have counseled an abusive man. This figure is noteworthy in its own right, for there are very few community-based services for men who batter their wives, and what services do exist seem to be poorly funded.[7] Thus pastors are among the few resources available to assist perpetrators of abuse.[8]

> The first battered women's shelter was opened in the United States in St. Paul, Minnesota, in 1974.

The Canadian data supplement the very limited data worldwide examining the experience of ministers in responding to women or men abused by family members.[9] Findings there suggest that a minority of evangelical clergy have substantial experience in this area, while most ministers report limited but ongoing counseling of abuse victims. It is critical not to exaggerate or minimize the counseling experience of clergy regarding family violence. While clearly clergy experience is no match for the prevalence of need in this area, pastors are an ongoing resource to battered women and abusive men, something our secular culture often fails to recognize. But how do they respond? What help do they offer?

A quick look at some social work literature or contemporary feminist writing would suggest that clergy are nearly always unhelpful, advising women to return to abusive home environments that threaten their physical or psychological health.[10] From this vantage point, clergy minimize women's pain and fear and teach their congregations the necessity of keeping the family together at all costs. Yet the data from scholarly research are far more complex than this partially informed view would suggest.

Opinions regarding how pastors respond to battered women who seek their counsel are marked by a lot of passion[11] but are informed by very limited empirical study.[12] A research project in which over one hundred evangelical ministers were interviewed found that *counseling* means something quite different to those trained in theology and professionals with social work, psychology or psychiatric degrees.[13] Ministers are less likely to set therapy goals, assess progress, evaluate interventions and refer to other community-based resources than workers who have secular credentials. On the other hand, clergy are more likely to be willing to see men and women at any time of the day or night, to schedule appointments at very short notice, to visit men or women in their own home, to tell about their own personal struggles, and to feel guilty when contact with a family does not lead to marked improvement. Somewhat surprisingly, clergy are often reluctant to offer specifically *spiritual* interventions, like Scripture reading or prayer. Perhaps they minimize its effectiveness to an abuse victim, or, more likely, they need guidance in how to read with, or pray for, a woman suffering abuse.[14]

> Every week in Hungary a woman is killed by her spouse.
> (<www.wave-network.org/articles/340.htm>)

While this research offers scant evidence that clergy admonish women to return home to unchanged abusive husbands, pastoral counselors are excessively optimistic that violent men *wish* to change their abusive ways and *will* cease their abusive behavior. Ministers often blame themselves for failing to engage a violent man in counseling or failing to bring reconciliation between a perpetrator and a victim. Since most clergy cling to the belief that violent relationships should be transformed, they feel discouraged and defeated when a violent relationship is terminated permanently. While evangelical clergy as a group are reluctant to recommend divorce, most do advise legal action when it becomes clear that an abusive man will not change his violent ways and when a woman's safety, as well as that of her children, is continually compromised.

Victims frequently report that simply hearing their pastor or religious leader condemn the abuse they have suffered aids in their healing. Sometimes such words are spoken in private as a pastor speaks words of comfort to a battered woman. Other times they are public words, preached in a sermon or taught in Sunday school. We suspect that if pastors realized how powerful their spiritual support for abused women actually could be, they would offer support more freely and more frequently. The dual impact of words of comfort for victims and words of condemnation for violent acts brings the healing balm of Gilead to people of faith who suffer abuse.

Offering several comforting Bible passages to a bruised woman validates her experience of pain and reminds her that God does not condone the violence she has suffered. She may feel that she deserves abuse. She may believe that this is her cross to bear. She may feel that she is not worthy to be treated like a human being. A wise pastor understands the extent of a victim's low self-esteem and applies the healing balm to her wounds just as the good Samaritan did to the hurt traveler. Validate her pain. Offer practical help. Soothe her broken spirit with God's words of comfort to her and God's word of rebuke to the perpetrator.

In Australia, hospital admissions for injuries related to abuse are 53 times more likely for those of Aboriginal descent. Aboriginal people (overwhelmingly women) are over 50 times more likely to be battered than non-Aboriginal people (<www.wa.gov.au/wpdo/dvpu/actionpln.html/introduction>)

As a spiritual shepherd, a pastor is uniquely positioned to bring comfort and offer challenge. But first he or she must understand the pain of the victim. Whether it is an abused woman seeking help on her own or a couple coming together, the knowledgeable pastor will ensure that the woman tells her own story in her own words, out of the presence of the man who intimidates her or has violated her body. Even if the couple arrives together, a pastoral counselor should ensure that in the assessment phase, each person has a private opportunity to recount their version of events. The experienced minister will ask appropriate questions, thereby making it safe for a woman to disclose in private her pain and vulnerability. She may initially say she has come for help because she is desperately unhappy. Asking a variety of questions about her life at home and work, the minister may hear her disclose violence or verbal abuse. While it is important not to assume violence in the life of every unhappy couple or unhappy woman, it is also critical not to assume the absence of violence simply because it has not been disclosed.

For most couples, religious or not, violence is a strongly guarded secret.[15] The woman may feel embarrassed, guilty, responsible for keeping her husband happy, responsible to keep the family together. She may have religious beliefs that inhibit her from saying anything unpleasant about her husband in unpleasant ways.[16] She may believe that the violence is her punishment for unkind words, spiritual immaturity or sinful actions. She may assume that since she married him, she must accept whatever he does to her. She may believe that God expects her always to turn the other cheek.[17] Sometimes she may feel that her life is next to worthless.

> In Bangladesh, throwing acid on a woman's face, so as to disfigure it, is so common that it is addressed in its own section of the penal code. (<www.unicef.org/pon97/women1.htm>)

A wonderful opportunity awaits the pastoral counselor who is sensitive to the suffering of a battered woman and knowledgeable about religious and secular resources to address her pain and malaise. The woman may need ongoing therapy that is beyond the pastor's expertise to provide. She may need legal counsel. She may need to flee to the safety of a transition house or other shelter.[18] She may need money or help with the children. Most certainly she needs a caring church community and a pastor who offers spiritual and emotional support, wise counsel and appropriate referral suggestions.

In a research study of evangelical youth ministers and their youth groups, teenagers claimed that their youth pastor could be described as a friend par excellence.[19] They sought out this pastor to help them sort out the sometimes conflicting demands of their parents, church and peers. Youth pastors themselves claimed that it was their interpersonal skills more than anything else that drew young men and women to them for counsel. They established credibility by being a friend—listening a lot, speaking a little. Many church youth reported that they rarely if ever discussed dating violence or family abuse within meetings held in the church. This is unfortunate, since many disclosed that their families had engaged in abusive behavior or that their dating relationships had at times been abusive.

The challenge to the spiritual shepherd, of adults or teens, is to simply acknowledge that violence in families is a pervasive problem and to offer help and healing for victims, model violence-free behavior and make their study a safe place for a person to disclose the pain and humiliation of battery.

At the end of the book we offer a list of resources that pastors can employ to address the needs of victims and perpetrators in their congregations or as they begin to think about how to raise awareness in their churches about these issues. It includes lists of helpful Scriptures, critical questions to ask a woman in crisis, helps for dealing with an abusive man, ways to identify essential community resources, and ways a congregation can get involved in helping address violence in the home.

As important as each of these lists is, perhaps the *most* useful list for pastors is the following one.

Questions to Ask Yourself When Responding to an Abused Woman

Keep this handy reference guide in your top desk drawer or in the portfolio you use when making notes during an interview session. You can glance at it to ensure that all the critical areas have been addressed in your response to a victim of wife abuse.

Am I sure that it is safe for this woman to return home?

Have I presented guidelines for what to do if her home is unsafe at any time?

Have I helped her develop a safety plan?

Have I validated her pain without being a judge?

Have I offered therapeutic options?

Have I made it clear that the church wants to be a safe place to disclose abuse?

Have I made it clear what resources are available in our church?

Have I made it clear what resources are available in our local community?

Have I condemned the abuse she has suffered in the language of the spirit?

Have I offered some spiritual help that is grounded in Scripture?

Have I prayed with her in a way that does not suggest that being a victim is her fault?

Have I offered practical help and support by seeking to understand what she needs at this point in her life?

Have I made it crystal-clear that she is welcome to come back whether or not she takes my advice?

Have I talked about what confidentiality means? Am I committed to keeping it?

Have I discussed the limits of pastoral confidentiality (e.g., mandatory reporting of child abuse)?

Have I determined whether the children are at risk? Whether the abuser is at risk?

Have I determined whether I, the pastoral counselor, am at risk?

4

Steeple to Shelter
Paving the Pathway

S everal older women make their way slowly from the parking lot toward the auxiliary door of the church building. It is Tuesday afternoon, and fifteen women have gathered to quilt, have a snack and pray for the women who are currently living in the local transition house. For several years now these seniors have donated the quilts they produce to the children who come with their moms to seek refuge at the shelter, often having fled from an abusive home with little preparation time. The quilters' goal: to ensure that every child who enters this publicly funded facility leaves with a handmade quilt. As a boy or girl cuddles in its warmth or gazes at its colorful patterns, the message will ring loud and clear: women who love God also love you.[1]

Victims of violence experience a multitude of practical and spiritual questions and dilemmas. They need multifaceted support—religious and secular, emotional and practical.[2] Yet workers trained in very different disciplines and ways of thinking often find it hard to cooperate to achieve a single goal.[3] It is not surprising, then, that secular workers, like staff in a transition house or social workers at a community agency, do not often refer religious clients to clergy. Why? They fear that the counsel offered in a pastoral study will thwart their clients'

healing journey. Simply put, they do not trust the advice of ministers. They believe that it will negate any progress achieved through therapeutic intervention. They think clergy would do more harm than good.

> In Luxembourg during 1997, 342 women and 363 children were offered assistance and housing through the Help Centres; 252 requests for admission had to be turned away.

It is also not surprising that clergy are very reluctant to refer their parishioners to secular sources of help. They fear that the counsel offered in a community health setting will break up the family and thwart a woman's spiritual development. They do not trust the advice of social workers or others trained in a discipline not specifically based on the Bible. They believe that the intervention of transition house staff will prevent reconciliation of an abusive man and his battered wife. They think secular social workers do more harm than good.

Violence is a multifaceted community problem with social, psychological, spiritual, legal and economic aspects. It cannot be eradicated by any one segment of society, however well intentioned, working in isolation from the broader community. Churches and clergy have a unique role to play in responding to the needs of abuse victims and their families. Faith communities can raise awareness of abuse and support violence-free family living by offering educational programs for men, women and children during the weekly routine of church life. Holding abusers accountable while offering hope for those desiring to change their violent behavior is another avenue of intervention by congregations.

Spiritual leaders have a valuable, distinct role in the fight to end violence in the family, but their practical and emotional assistance is far more effective when offered alongside the resources of other professionals and agencies. Working together, combining expertise and mission, augments the healing journey of victims and has the potential to transform the neighborhoods that churches serve. Sometimes clergy and police may cooperate. Sometimes it may be the transition house and a church women's group. Other times it may be workers at the mental health clinic and pastors. Or collaboration between school-teachers and youth leaders in the church, or initiatives involving a community center and a mission-oriented social action group of a congregation. Given that funding for public services is shrinking while many evangelical congregations are expanding their community mission statements, the message of the childhood song rings truer than ever: "The more we work together, together, together, the more we work together, the happier we'll be." Pooling our strengths and talents to respond compassionately to victims and to work toward a less violent society benefits everyone.

The rewards of cooperation notwithstanding, some very real challenges face religious and secular organizations thinking about *how* to begin to collaborate on the issue of woman abuse. The road to partnership does not necessarily involve endorsing all the interventions of another agency or group of professionals. But it does involve accepting and understanding the specific value and contribution of workers trained in many different disciplines. Ultimately it comes down to developing trust and respect among ministers and secular community workers, paving the way, as it were, for a pathway between the steeple and the shelter.[4]

> The United States surgeon general reports that domestic violence is the greatest single cause of injury among U.S. women, accounting for more emergency room visits than traffic accidents, muggings and rape combined.
> (<www.weaveinc.org/facts.html>)

One of the most effective ways faith communities are reaching out to women who have been abused involves the informal support network that operates within most congregations, where one woman meets another woman at her point of need. Women who meet to celebrate their faith and to be challenged to live it out reach out to other women in their family, women who are neighbors, women they work with or sisters in the faith, doing acts of kindness that say much louder than words, "I care about you and I want to help ease your pain." By providing childcare, a bed for the night, a referral suggestion, some groceries, transportation to a medical or legal appointment, or a listening ear, they form a circle of support around the battered woman who feels as if her world is caving in all around her. Such acts of mercy build a violated woman's sense of self and empower her to face the challenges ahead. They build the credibility of the caregiver and reinforce the significance of the mission of her faith community.

Ultimately, as one woman ministers to another woman, both caregiver and care receiver are empowered. This woman-centered spiritual empowerment helps meet the individual needs of hurting women even as it reinforces a sense of community connectedness within the church family. As women help each other, they do not demand that a battered wife sever all ties to her abusive husband forever, nor do they encourage her to return to a home where her physical or emotional health was in jeopardy. Rather, the circle of support offered by church women provides an abused and vulnerable woman with choices, therapeutic and practical options, destined to augment her journey toward healing and wholeness of body and spirit.

The Healing Journey
First and foremost, churches need to be safe places to disclose abuse.[5] Are they? While some women see their local congregation as a "safe haven," others report that "it's not a safe place to come . . . because nobody knows what to do with you."[6]

The first step on the road to recovery for women suffering abuse is to disclose the pain and humiliation they have endured to someone who is willing to listen in an environment that is safe and supportive. But before a woman can disclose her suffering, she has to interpret her past or present experiences as abusive. In other words, she has to name the pain and conflict as abuse. For the average Christian woman this is very difficult to do. And it poses several dilemmas for evangelical believers and their leaders.

Most clergy are reluctant to name the behavior of a violent man toward his wife for what it is; they would rather interpret the conflict as relational and the partners as equally responsible to seek help and resolution. Pastors prefer to see persistent verbal abuse as a couple's problem with communication and to downplay the economic and social dependency that a married woman often experiences. Ministers are slow to recognize unrestrained male power in a relationship, though they are usually decisive in their condemnation of violent physical outbursts.

Women believers, on the other hand, are far more likely than their leaders to understand the nature and severity of violence and to grasp the long-term consequences in the lives of victims. In part this is because Christian women have learned about the frequency and impact of wife abuse through the lives of their daughters, mothers and friends. Consequently, evangelical women are more likely to criticize the failure of the church and its leaders to respond compassionately to the problem than to condemn a woman's failure to leave an abusive relationship or to blame women for choosing their husbands poorly.

> Violence against women was declared a breach of human rights at the 1993 UN World Conference on Human Rights.

When abuse is addressed from the pulpit, in the pastoral study, in women's Bible-study classes, in Sunday school or in premarital workshops, those who have experienced its pain receive encouragement to come forward. The implicit message rings out: this church, or this pastoral study, is a safe place to recount your experience of being hurt. Giving violence a name and condemning it publicly is one tangible way that congregations and their leaders can respond directly to violence that occurs among women and men in their church family. The Sunday-morning sermon gives the average pastor a valuable opportunity to speak to victims, their families and the perpetrators in an environment where they are not singled out but can choose to respond. Research in various countries has indicated that large numbers of victims, approximately one in five, never disclose their experience of wife abuse until they are asked by an anonymous telephone interviewer to do so; they wait until they are asked.[7]

Once a disclosure of current abuse has been made, it is imperative to take immediate steps to ensure the physical and emotional safety of the victim and her children.[8] Does she have somewhere to go? Does she need transportation? The number-one priority must be to safeguard a woman's life, taking account of the possibility that the abusive man will seek retaliation.[9]

Once her safety is assured, a plethora of practical needs surface: the provision of emergency financial assistance, permanent lodging,[10] childcare, legal counsel, transportation, help for ongoing emotional needs, medical attention, spiritual counseling. Battered women who are Christian often feel that their spirit has been broken, that God does not care about their life, that they are worthless in every way. Among the unique challenges facing conservative Christian women are the enthusiasm among evangelicals for the intact nuclear family[11] and theological doctrines such as forgiveness, separation from the world, glorification of suffering, and instantaneous conversion.[12]

> There are nearly three times as many animal shelters in the United States as there are shelters for battered women and their dependent children.

One of the real challenges for evangelical pastors counseling abusive men is to be able to differentiate between their inauthentic pleas for the victim's forgiveness (or God's) and a genuine repentance that makes them accountable for the hurt they have caused, and its consequences, as well as accountable for changed behavior. No helping professional, however well intentioned, can set a time frame for the process of forgiveness and reconciliation. A victim who has heard an abuser say he is sorry many times before will need time and will need to see altered actions to believe that he is serious about living differently. Because evangelical men who are violent often want their pastor to encourage their victim to "forgive and forget," it is imperative that ministers understand the delicate terrain of a manipulative man's ways and a wounded woman's heart. This is not to suggest that evangelical clergy discount the power and potential of change in an abuser's life. But they must understand that many men who abuse their wives, whether they claim the name of Christ or not, claim to want to stop their violence but never do.

The healing journey for victims is long and arduous; many caregivers are required, and ongoing emotional support is needed for the transition from victim to survivor. Many Christian women who are battered would like assistance from both community agencies and their faith fellowship. Healing requires both the language of the spirit and the language of contemporary culture. Help that negates the support of others often thwarts the recovery process and augments pain and despair. The struggle to stop violence and to bring wholeness into the lives of its victims requires that the ideological fences between Christian and secular caregivers have many gates, enabling the smooth transition of hurting men and women to take advantage of the expertise of the physician, the pastor, the lawyer, the shelter worker and the psychologist. It is short-sighted to expect that one profession alone can respond single-handedly to what years of neglect and misuse have created.

Ensuring Care and Compassion in the Congregational Setting

Hurting men, women and children present the local church with an opportunity to put into practice what is preached from its pulpit, taught in its Sunday-school classes and studied in its home groups: that God cares about all human life and that congregations exist to bring that love to every person. Together God and Christian people are in the heart-mending business. But individuals must want the healing balm of Gilead to be applied to their wounds, and congregations must be prepared to offer it.

What does it mean to apply the healing balm of Gilead to our individual and collective hurts?

> "The harvest is past, summer is ended,
>   and we are not saved!"
> For the wound of the daughter of my people is my heart wounded,
>   I mourn, and dismay has taken hold of me.
> Is there no balm in Gilead?
>   Is there no physician there? (Jer 8:20-22 RSV)

> The Spirit of the Lord GOD is upon me,
>   because the LORD has anointed me;
> he has sent me to bring good news to the oppressed,
>   to bind up the brokenhearted . . .
>   to comfort all who mourn . . .
>   to give them a garland . . .
> the oil of gladness instead of mourning,
>   the mantle of praise instead of a faint spirit. . .
> Because their shame was double,
>   and dishonor was proclaimed as their lot,

therefore they shall possess a double portion;
everlasting joy shall be theirs. (Is 61:1-3, 7)

Go up to Gilead, and take balm. (Jer 46:11)

Applying the healing balm of Gilead involves proclaiming good news to the poor, for whom news is often bad; binding hearts that have been ripped apart by loneliness, disappointment and pain; comforting those who mourn; placing on the downcast a garment of praise; and offering everlasting joy to those who feel shame. Men and women bring to God and their church their brokenness, disappointment, shame, grief and despair, and in turn they are offered strength to fight, hope to endure, a sense of belonging—in essence, *love*. That is the biblical model. We bring to Christ our worn-down self and it is replaced, rejuvenated and renewed. The church, motivated and empowered by God's Spirit, is like a spiritual recycling center. Christianity is not a solo sport: it is togetherness, relationship, bonding under the umbrella of God's love, power and forgiveness. We offer our humanness and its associated frailty; God offers us the Comforter, peace and promise. We will never be alone.

> Twenty-four percent of Latin American and Caribbean women have been physically abused by a family member; wife abuse is worst in Guyana, Peru, Bolivia and Barbados.
> (<www.saartjie.co.za/march2000/vaw14.htm>)

When congregations catch a glimpse of what they have the potential to offer to hurting men and women—practical acts of kindness, lifelong compassion, hope that extends human capacity—they will never be the same.

How caring is your congregation? How caring are our denominations? How caring are we? There are scores of men, women and children who need God's touch, mediated by people of faith.

How Caring Is My Congregation?

Are Safety Mechanisms in Place?
☐ Have abuse victims been counseled to ensure that they have made

some advance preparations in case they need to leave their home quickly?

☐ Who can be called on short notice if there is an emergency facing a family in your congregation?

☐ Are there people in the congregation who are aware of the important safety issues for women and children in your area?

☐ Are there any members who are trained to provide emergency services?

☐ Does the church have a support group for victims of violence?

Do You Know the Transition Worker by Name?

☐ Does the pastor know the location of the nearest community shelter for battered women?

☐ Has the church established some contact with at least one worker at the shelter?

☐ If there are no community-based housing resources, has the congregation itself made some provision for emergency shelter?

Is Information Available in Safe Locations?

☐ Where is the safest location in your building to place information that abuse victims can look at in privacy (such as washrooms)?

☐ What information can be offered to women in immediate crisis or those in relationships that are sometimes abusive?

☐ Is a contact name and phone number provided on the literature?

Have You Asked the Shelter About Its Needs?

☐ Has a contact been made between the women's organizations in your church and the nearest shelter for battered women?

☐ Has the pastor ever called the shelter to inquire how the church might assist in its work (e.g., painting a room, moving a woman and her children, childcare, food treats at Christmas, spiritual counseling)?

Is Dating Violence Discussed in Youth Group?

☐ Has the youth pastor been informed about the prevalence and severity of dating violence even among church teens?

☐ Has information on dating violence been provided in a place where a teen can see it in privacy?

☐ Has the issue been raised from time to time in youth meetings, together with suggestions on how to respond to violence and how to help friends who have been abused?

Is Abuse Discussed in Premarital Counseling Programs?

☐ Is printed information on abuse (such as a brochure) given to all couples who undergo premarital counseling prior to their wedding?

☐ Are couples asked whether there has ever been an incidence of violence in their relationship?

☐ Are couples admonished to live violence-free lives and offered suggestions for dealing with anger and disappointment?

Have Sermons Condemned Abuse in the Home?

☐ Has the pastor ever preached a full message on abuse or family violence?

☐ Is the congregation reminded periodically that family living needs to be violence-free?

☐ When families are discussed, does the pastor mention that many families do not fit standard cultural and church ideals for family life?

No Place for Abuse

In many corners of the world the Christian family is considered sacred. It may be sacred—but is it *safe?*

Wounding and betrayal by someone who is (or has been) loved and trusted is a central feature of most forms of abuse. Like Jesus in the Garden of Gethsemane, who was seeking relief from the heat, shelter from the crowds and privacy to pray when Judas led the soldiers to his place of refuge, victims of battery are often assaulted in the very place where they have been taught to expect rest and renewal, the family home.

We have tried to draw attention to the inconsistency between the high priority evangelicals place on the family and the relative paucity of programs and resources for women and men experiencing family crisis. We believe that there is both a biblical mandate and sociological evidence to support violence-free family living so that women, men and children can live without fear. There is sound biblical—as well as social science—justification for listening to the voices of those who have been silenced and offering practical and emotional support in their search for wholeness. Offering hope and modeling compassion are the twin pillars on which Christians must respond to victims of violence within and beyond the walls of the faith community.

Our churches are no place for abuse. They ought to be well equipped with men and women of vision able and willing to apply the healing balm of Gilead to the wounds created by years of distress and suffering. Our homes are no place for abuse. They ought to contain believers, male or female, young or old, who resist physical force as a means of resolving disagreements and disappointments. The programs our congregations support and the ministries in which we are engaged ought to serve our constituencies and communities alike. Compassion is everyone's business. It needs to start at home. It needs to be encouraged in our congregations, the places where we seek guidance and strength.

May God grant us eyes to see the suffering of women and men around the world, ears to hear their sometimes silent cries for help, hearts that are moved to respond to their pain, and feet that are willing to accompany victims on their healing journey.

5

Searching
the Scriptures

The international student looked at me earnestly. "No one ever told me before that it was wrong to beat my wife," he said.[1] He had been raised in a culture where this behavior was slightly more acceptable than in America, and no one had bothered to condemn the practice.

He needed to understand that he could not defend himself by saying that it was simply a cultural issue. Violence against women is wrong for Christians in any culture. It is wrong because God's Word says so.

Why then is the problem so prevalent in Christian homes around the world? We believe that the Holy Spirit has power to restrain believers from sin, and therefore wife abuse should not be a problem among us. Part of the difficulty lies in our own ignorance.

We have failed to teach God's people what the Scriptures say about violence in general and about violence against women and children in particular. The psalmist observes that those who oppress others "are far from your law" (Ps 119:150). It is through God's law that a knowledge of sin is gained (Rom 3:20). Paul writes, "If it had not been for the law, I would not have known sin" (Rom 7:7). And with an understanding of that law, a new avenue is given for the Holy Spirit's work.

The power of the Spirit works not only to restrain evildoers but also to empower those who would obey the biblical command to deliver the helpless from the hand of the violent, to correct those of the family of faith who fall into sin, to set free those who are oppressed, to rebuke, admonish and instruct. Let us, the people of God, be instructed by the Scriptures. "Your word is a lamp to my feet and a light to my path" (Ps 119:105).

The Scriptural Witness

Both Old and New Testaments vigorously condemn violence of many sorts. A major theme is God's abhorrence and denunciation of violence. Violent behavior is a characteristic of sinful people and brings the judgment of God (Ps 11:5-6; Ezek 7:11; Joel 3:19; Amos 3:10; Obad 10; Hab 2:17; Zeph 1:9). Because of violence the earth was destroyed: "Now the earth was corrupt in God's sight, and the earth was filled with violence. . . . And God said to Noah, 'I have determined to make an end of all flesh, for the earth is filled with violence because of them'" (Gen 6:11, 13).

> By the word of your lips I have avoided the ways of the violent. (Ps 17:4)

Violence is associated with Satan (Ezek 28:16). It is accompanied by many sorts of wrong attitudes and conduct (Is 59:6-8; Jer 6:7; 22:17; Jon 3:8). The wicked drink "the wine of violence" (Prov 4:17), and the unfaithful "have a craving for violence" (Prov 13:2 NIV). Offenders develop a way of life sustained by their violence (Ps 73:4-8).

The Old Testament law made special provision to prevent violence within the home. Even a household slave was not to be treated abusively: "If a man hits a manservant or maidservant in the eye and destroys it, he must let the servant go free to compensate for the eye. And if he knocks out the tooth of a manservant or maidservant, he must let the servant go free to compensate for the tooth" (Ex 21:26-27).

Proverbs too addresses violence in the home.

Those who trouble their households will inherit wind. . . .
The fruit of the righteous is a tree of life,
    but violence takes lives away. (Prov 11:29-30)

Do not lie in wait like an outlaw against the home of the righteous;
    do no violence to the place where the righteous live. (Prov 24:15)

The New International Version offers an interesting alternative translation for a famous passage on marriage: " 'I hate a man's covering his wife with violence as well as with his garment,' says the LORD Almighty" (Mal 2:16 NIV mg.).

Patterns Accompanying Abuse
Characteristic patterns of abusers are noted in the Scriptures and draw comment. The violent devise injustice (Ps 58:2). "Their hearts plot violence" (Prov 24:2 NIV). Stalking and lying in wait are singled out for graphic descriptions.

In his arrogance, the wicked man hunts down the weak. . . .
He lies in wait near the villages;
    from ambush he murders the innocent,
    watching in secret for his victims.
He lies in wait like a lion in cover;
    he lies in wait to catch the helpless;
    he catches the helpless and drags them off in his net.
His victims are crushed, they collapse;
    they fall under his strength. (Ps 10:2, 8-10 NIV)

For other condemnations of stalking and harassment, see Psalm 17:11; 37:32; 56:5-6; 59:3; 140:5; Jeremiah 5:26; and Micah 7:2.

Abusive speech. The untruthfulness and evil speech of the violent is another basic theme (Ps 27:12; 52:2-4; 55:9; 140:11; Hos 12:1; Mic 6:12; Zeph 1:9).

My companion laid hands on a friend
    and violated a covenant with me
with speech smoother than butter,
    but with a heart set on war;
with words that were softer than oil,
    but in fact were drawn swords. (Ps 55:20-21)

Frequently physical or sexual abuse is accompanied by verbal abuse—one of the most common ways to exercise control over another.[2] As James remarked, the tongue can bless God or abuse one made in the image of God (Jas 3:9). Jesus spoke most poignantly of the damage that wrongful speech can inflict: "If you insult a brother or sister, you will be liable to the council; and if you say, 'You fool,' you will be liable to the hell of fire" (Mt 5:22). Why is it so hurtful to call another person stupid or crazy? Because it leaves that person feeling less than human, unable to think things through or to see issues clearly. "Death and life are in the power of the tongue, and those who love it will eat its fruits" (Prov 18:21). The psalmist prayed, "Let the heads of those who surround me be covered with the trouble their lips have caused" (Ps 140:9 NIV).

> The mouth of the righteous is a fountain of life but the mouth of the wicked conceals violence. (Prov 10:11)

Word-twisting is another technique of the abuser. Victims can be confused and overwhelmed by the adroit manner in which offenders distort what they have said and turn their own words against them. "All day long they twist my words; they are always plotting to harm me," cries the psalmist (Ps 56:5 NIV).

Another technique is to declare that what was said was only in jest: "What's the matter—can't you take a joke?" In this way the victim becomes even more bewildered as to what is really happening. She doubts her own sanity. Malachi 2:17 decries those who call right wrong and wrong right.

A further tool in an offender's arsenal is the threat. The psalmist notes, "Loftily they threaten oppression" (Ps 73:8). The mouth of the wicked "is full of curses and lies and threats; trouble and evil are under his tongue" (Ps 10:7 NIV). Threats can leave a victim constantly fearful, unable to develop a secure and confident attitude. The New Testament speaks of threats as the work of the wicked (Acts 4:21, 29; 9:1) and commands believers not to threaten those in their own household (Eph 6:9).

Abuse hurts the abuser. We are told that batterers abuse those in their family because in this manner they achieve the results they are seeking. Frequently the abuser convinces his family that his treatment of them is in response to their own misdeeds. Victims are humiliated, degraded, shamed, reproached, made to feel inadequate and guilt-ridden.

Thus they are coerced into compliance with the perpetrator's wishes. Whether by physical, sexual or emotional abuse, the abuser is

> The violence of the wicked will drag them away, for they refuse to do what is right.
> (Prov 21:7 NIV)

able to exercise control over the household. The harm done to individual members is ignored or justified. Frequently reproach falls on the victims rather than on the offender. If they had only been more prayerful, more submissive, more careful not to arouse anger, the problem would not have arisen. But this is not where the Bible puts the responsibility. The Bible says the abuser is at fault. "In your hearts you devise wrongs; your hands deal out violence on earth" (Ps 58:2).

Often well-meaning Christians assume that what happens within the household is a matter between God and the offender. We fail to understand that abuse hurts the abuser.

> The trouble he causes recoils on himself;
>> his violence comes down on his own head. (Ps 7:16 NIV)

> They say, . . . "Let us lie in wait for blood;
>> let us wantonly ambush the innocent." . .

> Yet they lie in wait—to kill themselves!
>> and set an ambush—for their own lives!
>>> (Prov 1:11, 18; see also Prov 19:19)

The Bible tells us further that abuse hinders the prayers of perpetrators. The prophet Isaiah addressed those who were engaged in services of prayer and fasting. Although they had gathered together before the Lord and professed true faith, their supplications were to no avail: "You fast only to quarrel and to fight and to strike with a wicked fist. Such fasting as you do today will not make your voice heard on high" (Is 58:4). The thought is repeated in 1 Peter 3:7, where husbands are instructed to treat their wives considerately "so that nothing may hinder your prayers."

Many Christian congregations do little to alleviate the sufferings of abused family members. They must remember that the abuser also is harmed by their inaction. That in itself should constitute a call to Christian action. Allowing an offender to perpetuate the sin can only further harm him or her. The Bible tells us to correct those who are in error and restore them to God's ways.

God's Response to Violence Against Women and Children

God hears the prayers of the oppressed and desires that they experience release (2 Sam 22:3-4). The Bible records many cries for deliverance. The cry of the abused Israelite slaves came up before God (Ex 3:7, 9), and the great salvation story of the Old Testament is of their deliverance.

> You hear, O LORD, the desire of the afflicted;
>> you encourage them, and you listen to their cry,
> defending the fatherless and the oppressed,
>> in order that man, who is of the earth, may terrify no more.
>> (Ps 10:17-18 NIV)

The psalmist prays, "Deliver me from those who work evil; from the bloodthirsty save me" (Ps 59:2; see also 139:19; 140:1, 5; Hab 1:2-9). The great psalm affirming the power of Scripture (Ps 119) is full of appeals for deliverance from violence and oppression:

> Redeem me from human oppression,
>> that I may keep your precepts. (v. 134)
> Look on my misery and rescue me,
>> for I do not forget your law. (v. 153)
> Many are my persecutors and adversaries. (v. 157)
> Princes persecute me without cause. (v. 161)
> I hope for your salvation, O LORD. (v. 166)

A more sustained prayer is found in Psalm 140:

> Deliver me, O LORD, from evildoers;
>> protect me from those who are violent,
> who plan evil things in their minds
>> and stir up wars continually.
> They make their tongues sharp as a snake's,
>> and under their lips is the venom of vipers.

Guard me, O LORD, from the hands of the wicked;
>   protect me from the violent
>   who have planned my downfall.
The arrogant have hidden a trap for me,
>   and with cords they have spread a net,
>   along the road they have set snares for me. (vv. 1-5)

But our God is a God of action. David praises the Lord for answered prayer in delivering him from the violent (2 Sam 22:49; Ps 18:48). God's mercy and power liberate and defend victims of cruelty and aggression. "The Lord works vindication and justice for all who are oppressed" (Ps 103:6). " 'Because the poor are despoiled, because the needy groan, I will now rise up,' says the LORD. 'I will place them in the safety for which they long'" (Ps 12:5). The same promises of protection are found in Isaiah 54:11-17 and 60:17-18.

In 1992 U.S. Roman Catholic bishops announced that "women should not consider themselves religiously bound to remain in abusive relationships."[3] The bishops said that an area that particularly concerns them as church leaders is the way biblical passages encouraging wives to be submissive to their husbands have been taken out of context to justify spouse abuse. Abused women say, "I can't leave this relationship. The Bible says it would be wrong." Abusive men say, "The Bible says my wife should be submissive to me." They take the biblical text and distort it to support their right to batter, the bishops said. The bishops said that violence against women is never justified and that the parish must be a place where abused women and men who batter can come for help.[4]

The Protection of Children

The protection of children is a theme that is sounded frequently in the Bible (for example, Deut 14:29; Job 31:17; Mt 18:2-6; Jas 1:27), but it is often forgotten when the church is informed of an abusive situation. One-third of all abused women are battered during their pregnancy, with the majority of blows being delivered to the abdomen and breasts. The March of Dimes identifies prenatal abuse as one of the leading causes of birth defects. Other results include premature birth, miscarriage, learning difficulties and emotional problems. Although the Bible speaks of prenatal influence, this is usually disregarded. Churches will do much to protect the unborn from the hands of an abortionist but little to protect the unborn from batterers.

The list of emotional, psychological and spiritual problems that can develop in those who witness the abuse of their mothers is even more appalling. When Christians hesitate to intervene in a home, even when they are aware of violence, they ignore the very grave consequences. According to the Massachusetts Department of Youth Services, children who witness violence in their home are

□ six times more likely to commit suicide

□ twenty-four times more likely to commit sexual assault

□ 50 percent more likely to abuse drugs and alcohol

□ 74 percent more likely to commit crimes against others[5]

Over 60 percent of murderers between the ages of fifteen and twenty-one are incarcerated for having killed their mother's abuser.

Where is the church's concern for those of the household of faith? Do we not have a responsibility to intervene before sons are driven to such desperate acts?

> From the perspective of the cross, violence against women is exposed as sin that divides humankind, violates the dignity of God's creation, abuses power, and obstructs the gospel message of salvation and freedom.[6]

God's purpose is to deliver the victim from the hand of the violent, and to this all who love God are called. We have been tardy in responding: "Again I saw all the oppressions that are practiced under the sun: Look, the tears of the oppressed—with no one to comfort them! On the side of their oppressors there was power—with no one to comfort them" (Eccles 4:1). How tragically true is this of substantial portions of the evangelical community when it comes to violence against women. But we cannot escape the divine directive:

Thus says the LORD:

Execute justice in the morning,
>   and deliver from the hand of the oppressor
>   anyone who has been robbed,
or else my wrath will go forth like fire,

and burn, with no one to quench it,
      because of your evil doings. (Jer 21:12)

Of God's intention for Solomon's reign it was written:

For he delivers the needy when they call,
      the poor and those who have no helper.
He has pity on the weak and the needy,
      and saves the lives of the needy.
From oppression and violence he redeems their life;
      and precious is their blood in his sight. (Ps 72:12-14)

And to those who had ruined the sanctity of the holy fast by their
violence, Isaiah gave the Lord's oracle:

Is not this the kind of fasting I have chosen:
to loose the chains of injustice
      and untie the cords of the yoke,
to set the oppressed free
      and break every yoke? (Is 58:6 NIV)

Jeremiah maintained that to know God was to do his work in
defending those in need (Jer 22:15-16). Those who profess Christ
have an obligation to do his work.

Thus says the LORD: Act with justice and righteousness, and deliver
from the hand of the oppressor anyone who has been robbed. And do
no wrong or violence to the alien, the orphan, and the widow, or shed
innocent blood in this place. (Jer 22:3)

Let us give careful heed to what the Scriptures so clearly teach.

6

Man & Woman

Dimensions of Their Union

To gain deeper understanding of the relationship between men and women, we must begin with the book of Genesis, since the Bible is our only infallible rule of faith and practice. In a marvelously poetic story we are told of a wise God who made all things and saw that they were good—that is, until it comes to the creation of humankind. Then God saw that it was "not good" that the man should be alone. Humanity, made in God's image, must be relational as God is relational, sharing mutual love and joy and wholeness.

In the creation story, male and female are made equally in the image of God, as woman is drawn from the very substance of man, to share his dreams, his intellect, his emotions, his spirituality. Greek tradition held that woman was made of an inferior substance, a cruel trick of the gods to despoil the potential of man. Hebrew tradition tells of a helper who is of a shared essence, a blessed gift from the true and living God. Woman was bestowed to save man from loneliness.

The creation of the family is celebrated with Adam's song: "This at last is bone of my bones and flesh of my flesh." The two became one flesh, naked and unashamed, joyful in their togetherness, tender and caring in a newfound relationship.

This garden relationship is still possible for those who seek it according to God's guidelines, as husbands and wives are able to share themselves freely. The Song of Solomon contains a recurring image of a garden as a place of love-making and delight (Song 4:12, 15-16; 5:1; 6:2). This walled garden accommodates two people deeply committed to each other. There they may walk together as did the first pair (Amos 3:3). The deeply satisfying and exclusive bond is intended to last throughout life, a renewable resource.

> Drink deep from your own cistern,
>   flowing water from your own well.
> Should your springs be scattered abroad,
>   streams of water in the streets?
> Let them be for yourself alone,
>   and not for sharing with strangers.
> Let your fountain be blessed,
>   and rejoice in the wife of your youth,
>   a lovely deer, a graceful doe.
> May her breasts satisfy you at all times;
>   may you be intoxicated always by her
>   love. (Prov 5:16-19)

The Bible speaks of marital love as a world of wonder.

> Three things are too wonderful for me;
>   four I do not understand:
> the way of an eagle in the sky,
>   the way of a snake on a rock,
> the way of a ship on the high seas,
>   and the way of a man with a girl. (Prov 30:18-19)

We are given a sublime picture of the pinnacles of married love in the Song of Solomon. Each of the two partners seeks and cherishes a communion of mind, soul and body. They perceive the beauty of one another's body, the joy of being made one. Like Adam and Eve, they are naked and unashamed, ready to share their inmost souls.

Affirmed as a person by her husband ("his speech is most sweet," Song 5:16), the bride is free to communicate her thoughts, experiences and emotions, as does the bridegroom. Their world is marked by a shared intimacy that is possible only because each is confident in the other. There can be no hint of abuse, control, humiliation, betrayal, belittling or manipulation.

Such union grows only in the garden of mutual respect and sharing. A wife who is considered less than her husband cannot bring her full self to the marital union, nor can the husband know the joy of full communion.

> Your rounded thighs are like jewels,
>   the work of a master hand.
> Your navel is a rounded bowl
>   that never lacks mixed wine.
> Your belly is a heap of wheat,
>   encircled with lilies.
> Your two breasts are like two fawns,
>   twins of a gazelle. (Song 7:1-3)

God's plan for sexual union involves the two participants' total being. They have a new awareness of all of the beauty around them, and they burst into rapturous poetic expression.

How is it that this remarkable description of marital love is so often read devotionally? Why do people use it to guide them to an adoration and love of Christ as the heavenly bridegroom? Hymns and Christian devotional literature throughout the centuries have been heavily dependent on the language and concepts of the Song of Solomon, and this is no mistake. The spiritual in our nature lies very close to the sexual. The union depicted in the Song is exalted to the highest pinnacle of human lovemaking. What better way to meditate on our seeking of God than in the sublime language with which Solomon's song vests human love?

The Bible makes a strong differentiation between sex that enriches the human spirit and that which degrades it. Scripture speaks candidly of the sordid uses to which sex can be put: manipulation and exploitation, violence and aggression. It can debase the relationship, demean the person and violate the soul. Victims can be left with wounds that will last the rest of their lives; and abusers, if they take responsibility for their deeds, are left with intolerable guilt. If sex is so powerful that it can bind two people into one flesh, then it must be used reverently and with great caution.

"Let marriage be held in honor by all, and let the marriage bed be kept undefiled," urges the writer of the epistle to the Hebrews (13:4). One perpetrator used this scripture to persuade his timid young bride of the legitimacy of violent sex. She consented reluctantly, convinced that she was obeying a biblical injunction; but extensive gynecological surgery was necessary to repair the damage that was done.[1]

This Bible passage was not given to justify sexual abuse within marriage. *Timios*, the Greek adjective used here to describe marriage, means not only "esteemed" or "honored" but also conferring honor, esteem or respect. We might alternatively translate the passage: "Marriage confers honor on all, and the marriage bed should be untainted."

Tragically, there is much that can spoil a blessed union. As the passage goes on to point out, fornication and adultery destroy the bond and create a terrible breach of trust. But there are many other kinds of betrayal that can rupture the bond. To dishonor the body, mind or sensibilities of one's mate cannot fail to flaw the union. The apostle Paul understood this:

> For this is the will of God, your sanctification: that you abstain from fornication; that each one of you know how to control your own body in holiness and honor, not with lustful passion, like the Gentiles who do not know God; that no one wrong or exploit a brother or sister in this matter, because the Lord is an avenger in all these things, just as we have already told you beforehand and solemnly warned you. For God did not call us to impurity but in holiness. Therefore whoever rejects this rejects not human authority but God, who also gives his Holy Spirit to you. (1 Thess 4:3-8)

Abuse of any kind—whether verbal, emotional, physical or sexual—destroys true intimacy. Within the marriage bed honor and holiness are essential. First Thessalonians 4:4 may alternatively be translated "that each of you know how to hold a spouse in holiness and honor," since *skeuos* (literally, "vessel") means both one's own body and one's spouse. Demanding sexual acts that are demeaning, offensive or repugnant does not respect the other. It is to defraud one's partner of her or his dignity.

There are many kinds of sexual abuse: Perhaps the most common form of abuse in Christian homes is coercion. Taking St. Paul's dictate that neither party should defraud the other of sexual fulfillment (1 Cor 7:5), many husbands demand sexual submission of unwilling wives. Many women are defrauded by the sexual treatment that they receive—whether rape, coercion or manipulation. They are not allowed free choice in the relationship and may end up as toys, sex objects or slaves. Paul is clear that each partner holds power over the body of the other, and each is to show consideration for the other (1 Cor 7:3-4).

Women are frequently demeaned, even in Christian circles, by sexual harassment. Yet the church is called to repudiate all obscenity (Eph 5:4; Col 3:8). Dirty jokes are not funny—indeed they can inflict far more harm than we might imagine.

Rape, even in marriage, is reprehensible and receives condemnation in the stories of the Old Testament. In 1 Corinthians rapists are singled out as being unworthy of the kingdom of God. Though usually concealed by translation, the word *harpax* is used for one who commits rape (1 Cor 5:10-11; 6:10). The King James Version comes the closest in rendering the word "rapacious." In context, this word occurs in conjunction with perpetrators of other sorts of sexual sin. They are not acceptable members of the household of God!

Betrayal of Trust

Many a child in a Christian household has known the agony of betrayal by those they trusted. Aunts, uncles, grandparents, siblings and parents have all been guilty of manipulating naive children for their own sexual gratification. All too often Christian sentiments and twisted Scriptures are utilized to serve the offender's purpose.

> If any of you should put a stumbling block *[cause to sin, shock, fill with disgust]* before one of these little ones who believe on me, it would be better for you if a great millstone were fastened around your neck and you were drowned in the depth of the sea. (Mt 18:6)

When the perpetrator is a Christian or uses religious arguments, the child becomes even more confused and often carries scars that remain through his or her life.

Any kind of abuse destroys the joyous spontaneity that should characterize marital union. Some women's shelters have pointed their clients to a psalm that well expresses the feelings of a victim:

> It is not enemies who taunt me—
> > I could bear that;
> It is not adversaries who deal insolently with me—
> > I could hide from them.
> But it is you, my equal,
> > my companion, my familiar friend,
> with whom I kept pleasant company;
> > we walked in the house of God with the throng. (Ps 55:12-14)

Gone are the delight and the trust that must be basic components of sexual intimacy at its most profound level.

7

Does the Suffering
of an Abused Woman
Bring Salvation
to Her Husband?

First Peter Revisited

R ecently a Catholic woman went to confession and poured out
to the priest a story of the abuse she was enduring.[1] He
encouraged her to go home and demonstrate a more loving
attitude toward her husband in order to win him to Christ, according to
the instructions in 1 Peter 3:1-6. The priest concluded "You really have
nothing to fear. If he kills you, you'll be a martyr in heaven."

Another woman was wakened at two in the morning by furious
blows wielded by her husband with a child's metal tricycle.[2] In terror
she consulted a popular women's speaker and was told to return to
her husband in order that her gentleness might lead him to conversion. Again, the text was 1 Peter 3:1-6. Underlying the advice was the
assumption that her suffering would result in his salvation.

First Peter 3:1-6 is often used to argue that women should endure domestic abuse heroically in order to convert their husbands. In point of fact, the passage addresses spousal abuse only to insist that husbands honor their wives as equals and that failure to do so will obstruct the abuser's prayer life. It is significant that New Testament calls for wifely submission are always constructed within a framework of mutuality (1 Cor 7:3-5; Eph 5:18-33; Col 3:13-19; 1 Pet 2:16-3:8) and always accompanied by specific directives to prevent abuse on the part of the husband (Eph 5:28-29; Col 3:19; 1 Pet 3:7).

A Letter to the Persecuted

First Peter is essentially a letter addressed to those whom others viewed with hostility simply because they were Christians (1 Pet 4:13-16). The treatise deals with those who "are reviled for the name" and who suffer as Christians (1 Pet 4:14, 16). In the early church there were times when even the name of Christ was enough to bring condemnation to death.

Christians were under a great cloud of suspicion, beset by false rumors throughout the Roman Empire. One need only think of the allegations that were leveled by Nero at the followers of Christ as perpetrators of incest, impiety, atheism, hatred of humanity and sedition. Their refusal to worship the traditional gods was construed as a danger to the state, and their disengagement from civic activities (many directly related to rituals of worship) supposedly proved they had no concern for assuming civil responsibility.

Therefore it was all the more necessary that Christians demonstrate their law-abiding proclivities in every other way possible. Loyalty to established rulers and good citizenship are stressed (1 Pet 2:13-14). All believers are called to behavior that will belie the opposition of the critics (1 Pet 2:12, 15).

There is a threefold call to submission in 1 Peter: (1) by citizens to properly appointed authorities (2:13-16), (2) by slaves to masters (2:18) and (3) by wives to husbands (3:1-2).

Proper definition is important, as some faith groups insist that the Bible demands wifely obedience regardless of the husband's behavior. The word for submission is *hypotassō*, over against a somewhat related term, *hypakouō*. The latter denotes obedience and in 1 Peter is applied to a believer's obedience to Christ (1:2, 14, 22). But *hypotassō*, rather than *hypakouō*, is applied to wives in 1 Peter 3:1, 5 as well as in Ephesians 5:22, Colossians 3:18 and Titus 2:5. *Hypotassō* is rendered "accept" (NRSV) or "submit yourselves" (NIV, KJV, 2:13) but has a wide semantic range. We find implied synonyms in 2:17 ("honor," "love," "fear"). The literal meaning "to place oneself under," or in military parlance, "to draw up behind," developed other meanings: to serve as an ally, to attach to, identify or associate with, adhere to, or relate in such a way as to make meaning.[3] The term had also the sense of loyalty and of orderly and accountable behavior.

In view of Peter's resolute insistence that obedience must be yielded to God rather than human beings (Acts 4:19; 5:29), one can hardly construe a believer's submission to civil authorities as absolute obedience. In no way can duty to state be placed higher than the dictates of God or of individual conscience. Rather there is a call to Christians to comply within the structures necessary for the peaceful functioning of society and to discharge all rightful obligations of citizenship.

Since Christians met for worship in private houses, the household was particularly open to the inspection of those curious about the new faith. This occasioned special instruction to members of the family, especially women and slaves.

Peter's Words to Slaves

The directive to wives (1 Pet 3:1-6) follows an instruction to slaves and a discussion of Christ's passion. The arrangement of segments is noteworthy. First come advice and consolation for slaves who are mistreated (2:18-20), followed by the observation that Christ too was abused and mistreated (2:21-25). The juxtaposition has led many to conclude that it is the will of God for both slaves and women to suffer as Christ suffered. The passion of Christ is a recurring theme throughout the epistle (1 Pet 1:18-20; 2:21-25; 3:18—4:1; 4:13; 5:1), with assurance to believers that his sacrificial death had procured their salvation and that he would keep their souls safe if it became necessary for them to suffer "for the sake of the name."

What were the challenges faced by a slave with an unbelieving master? The slave might deny Christ, run away or endure savage mis-treatment. To be beaten for unruly conduct brought no reward from God, but suffering for the sake of one's faith was another matter (2:20). Even in the later church as well as among pagans, a sound drubbing was considered highly effective in bringing the religious views of a slave into accord with those of the master.[4] First Peter makes a careful differentiation between the constructive behavior that should be expected from a Christian slave and the abuse he or she might suffer in consequence of professing faith in Christ.

A slave might ordinarily appeal to a magistrate if he or she was the victim of excessive brutality. During a period of intense persecution, however, such an action would further jeopardize the life of the slave. If the conversion to Christianity had been kept a secret, an official investigation might bring the fact to light, with disastrous conse-quences.

Peter's Words to Wives

In the same way, a woman might find it advisable to be judicious about revealing her allegiance to Christ. Christian women were under particular criticism from many quarters. During a persecution it was not unknown for a husband to deliver his Christian wife to the authorities.[5] A wife in such circumstances might do well to reveal her spiritual convictions only after the husband had been won over by her grace-filled lifestyle. According to 1 Peter 3:1-4, submissive wives should demonstrate exemplary conduct, and their style of dress should avoid characteristics commonly thought to be most aggravat-ing to husbands. Braided hair was considered enormously seductive and gold the mark of a harlot.

The call for slaves to submit can be seen as a challenge to render responsible and constructive behavior even in unjust circumstances, but not to surrender their faith or the dictates of their conscience. The call for wifely submission is significant because in the most critical area the wife is encouraged to stand her ground. Classical literature abounds in expressions of the aggravation that men felt at the free practice of women's religion. They found the cults of women noisy, depraved, debauched, abandoned, ridiculous and disgusting. By contrast, the Christian wife is to demonstrate her convictions with silence instead of clamor, decorum instead of depravity, faithfulness instead of promiscuity. Instead of worshiping the gods of her husband's family as was expected of a dutiful member of a household, she aims instead to win him over to her faith.

Her submission was not a renunciation of her own spiritual capacity or conscience, any more than was the decree to be subject to governmental authorities. "Submission" here involves scrupulous fulfillment of all legitimate obligations of marriage while upholding freedom to serve Christ. The aim is not subordination but conversion, not by enabling what is wrong but by persisting in what is right.

The women addressed have made a radical decision about their personal faith. As daughters they were expected to worship the household gods of their fathers' families. The text presupposes that these women will make their own decisions about religious matters. A *sine manu* marriage, literally "without hand," would make them still members of their father's household, still bound to the familial religion. A *cum manu* marriage transferred a woman's guardianship to her husband and thereby transferred her allegiance to the gods of his hearth. While the text seems to favor a woman's alignment with her husband rather than with her birth family, personal faith lies quite outside. The directive is issued to women whose husbands disapprove of their spiritual convictions, and to these a wife should hold fast (1 Pet 5:9). Her conduct should be irreproachable, but her faith is her own; and she should be fearless in maintaining it.

Curiously enough, the word *hypakouō* ("obey") is used to describe Sarah's conduct. Her outstanding obedience appears to have been in following her husband as he left the comforts of a brilliant civilization to follow God's call into an unknown land among an alien people. Her life was fraught with incredible difficulties, but she persisted as a devoted wife who shared her husband's call. Women find it particularly difficult to be uprooted and to sever familiar ties. To find oneself among people who do not share one's personal faith is even worse. The thought of Sarah's journey of faith might give great encouragement to women living as strangers in an alien land (1 Pet 1:1) or embarking on missionary journeys. Peter's own wife accompanied him on his travels and shared his labors in the gospel (1 Cor 9:5).

The writer's allusion to Sarah's obedience creates a perplexity. Does it refer to the sorry episode in which Abraham cravenly denied that he was married to her and allowed the king of Egypt to take her into his household? Abraham demonstrated a flagrant lack of faith and obedience to God's promise (compare 1 Pet 3:1) in requiring his wife to risk life and virtue for his own self-preservation (Gen 12:12). Confronted with a life-threatening situation in a hostile alien environment, she had little recourse but to comply. Sarah could hope only in God to deliver her (1 Pet 3:5), a deliverance that came by the affliction of Pharaoh and his house with plagues (Gen 12:17). She dared not reveal her identity as wife of Abraham and a pilgrim who espoused a new faith. Faced with imminent danger especially for her husband, she remained silent. In time Pharaoh became aware of her identity and set her free to pursue the calling of God.

Abraham appears as culpable in both this story and in the similar episode with Abimelech (Gen 20:1-18). Abimelech's household is visited with sterility, and the truth of Sarah and Abraham's relationship is revealed (Gen 20:3-7, 18). By complying with her husband's request, Sarah brought misfortune on others and reproach on Abraham (Gen 12:10-20; 20:2-18). Far from a blessing to all nations, his infidelity made him a curse.

The relationship of Sarah and Abraham was more mutual than a cursory reading of the preceding text might envisage. Certainly in the biblical account she accompanies him as a faithful companion on his journey of faith. David Balch maintains that "I Peter 3:6 teaches that wives must fear God (cp. 2:17; 3:2) and not be terrified of those in house or city who oppose their faith (cp. 3:14)."[6]

The observation that Sarah "obeyed" her husband must be contrasted with God's command to Abraham to heed and obey his wife (Gen 21:12). The Genesis account emphasizes her insistence on a course of action that her husband strongly opposes. God tells Abraham that he is to follow his wife's bidding. The episode is another unhappy one: Sarah sees the adolescent Ishmael engaging in behavior that threatens the newly weaned Isaac. A Hebrew verb *(ṣḥq)* sometimes having sexual and abusive connotations is used to describe the older brother's conduct (Gen 21:9; 26:8; 39:14, 17; Ex 32:6; 2 Sam 2:14; compare also Prov 26:19). Sarah demands that he be removed from the home. Interestingly, the apostle Paul cites that demand as Scripture (Gal 4:30). First Peter 3:6 tells us that Christian women as daughters of Sarah should be *fearless in doing what is right.*

As a deterrent to possible abusive behavior by believing husbands, 1 Peter now gives a set of instructions outlining the norms for Christian family living. The section (3:7) begins with "in the same way," connecting the man's submission to that of the wife (3:1-6), to counsel for household slaves (2:18-25) and to the more general earlier commands (2:13, 17).

The text, however, calls for husbands to honor their spouses as joint heirs. An heir is one who receives an inheritance and manages it. The concept of a woman as joint heir with her husband would have been radical in both Jewish and Roman society. Here women are presented as coheirs of "life-giving grace," equal in the sight of God and of the believing community.

The allusion to the wife as a weaker vessel seems to be an acknowledgment that men possess greater physical strength and should therefore refrain from using it abusively. The husband who lived "according to knowledge," affirming his wife in honor and equality, would find power in his prayers. Abuse or denigration would bring an obstruction to their prayers (3:7), a deterrent to the husband's spiritual life and growth. Here we find an echo of Isaiah's warning that God will not hear the prayers of the violent (Is 58:4). Enabling human beings to perpetuate their sin certainly does not open the doors of salvation to them (1 Pet 3:7). Like others, a woman may suffer for her faith; but brutality at the hands of her husband is another matter.

The mandates of 1 Peter 2:18—3:8 are not a blanket call for slaves or women to endure abuse. Suffering that allows a perpetrator to continue abusive conduct can never be redemptive. Rather it brings an enablement of sin that is damaging to the soul of both perpetrator and victim. In many of today's societies there are legitimate avenues of recourse for a laborer or a wife to gain relief from abusive treatment. Where there is legal redress for abuse, patient endurance is more likely to be seen as codependence than as exemplary conduct.

Sometimes victims are encouraged to endure abuse as Jesus did. We need to make a differentiation between his voluntary suffering to procure our redemption and his ability in other situations to defend himself against verbal abuse (Mk 3:22-30; Jn 8:48-59) and the threat of violence (Lk 4:28-30; Jn 8:59; 10:31-39). Being a doormat in an abusive situation is *not* following the example of Jesus.

In some situations women submit to abuse because they feel that they are being punished for some misdeed. This is to deny the power and efficacy of Christ's sacrifice. He bore our sins so that we might be free from them (1 Pet 2:24). Women must accept the deliverance that is so freely offered.

> Carol Adams suggests that a woman be encouraged to "let Jesus off the cross. We are a resurrection people. Let yourself off the cross. Your suffering should be over too. Because of Jesus you do not need to die to experience the meaning and power of resurrection. If you don't get off the cross, however, you very well may die."[7]

Daughters of Sarah

We must help women understand that they have the God-given right to make moral and spiritual decisions. Women must answer to God and not to their husband, their relatives or their faith community. Like Sarah they may be called to strike out in a new direction. Like Sarah they may find it necessary to insist that their children not live in an actual or potentially abusive situation. Like Sarah they must act on their concern for the safety of their children and their own. And like Sarah they may find God's affirmation when they reach a conclusion that conflicts with their husband's wishes.

How may these passages, written to people caught in persecution for the faith, be applied to present-day situations that involve no oppression for one's faith? First, believers must demonstrate a lifestyle that can withstand criticism.

Second, many biblical passages condemn violence, verbal and sexual abuse. Christian women can profitably be directed toward passages that call on communities of faith as well as victims to take positive steps to stop the wrongdoing.

Third, God calls husband and wife, as coheirs, to live joyfully with respect and love for each other. A distortion of this balance brings obstruction not only of effective prayer but of true communion in marriage. Jesus specifically deplored one person's exercising dominance over another (Mt 20:25-28; Mk 10:42-45) and declared that it hinders intimacy (Jn 15:15). All believers are called to unity of spirit, sympathy, love for one another, a tender heart and a humble mind.

Christianity is based on mutuality, interdependence and equality. Shared decision-making is the pattern sanctified by Scripture and proven effective in human experience.

8

A Concern for
the Christian Family

The Dangers of Idolization
& Idealization

An evangelical believer, depressed to the point of suicide, had managed to leave a seriously abusive marriage. Friends had insisted on attempts at reconciliation, and the wife of a Christian therapist announced, "It will be such a feather in my husband's cap if he can get you two back together!"[1] There was little concern to address the situation that had led to the wife's life-threatening state, but much eagerness to keep up appearances and make things look right to the wider evangelical community. The hypocrisy threw the woman into even deeper despair.

The Bible tells us to live honestly in the sight of all people (Rom 12:17). Integrity is better than deceitful appearances.

Modern Christians have sometimes idealized and even idolized the family. But keeping the family together is not the highest goal of the Christian faith. The Bible tells of God's work through families even though they were deeply troubled. As in Bible times, abuse knows no faith boundaries; it occurs both within and beyond the faith community.

After an abusive incident a missionary child asked, "Are we going to go downstairs and pretend to be a happy Christian family again?"[2] The pretense of being a happy Christian family only confuses and compounds the tragedy of abuse against women and children. To deny, minimize or ignore the problem obstructs the work of the Holy Spirit. The Scriptures offer the hope of healing for troubled families, but it requires honesty, faith, hard work and the support of the believing community.

As people of faith we hate to admit that the problem exists in our midst. As a result we offer few resources to people in our own churches, whether the problem is incest, rape, battering, intimidation or verbal, sexual or emotional abuse. We hesitate to believe the victim who summons up enough courage to seek help in the church. Often our biggest priority is making sure that no one knows, that the behavior of a supposedly model church member is not revealed, that the status quo is not shaken.

Biblical Patterns

The Bible is devastatingly honest. Biblical texts make no effort to deny or conceal sad realities. Many of the families described in the Bible are perfectly awful, not to mention incredibly dysfunctional. Cain kills Abel, Joseph's brothers sell him into slavery, Jacob practices deceitful stratagems on his father, brother and father-in-law and barely escapes with his life. Abraham and Isaac both allow their wives to be inducted into other men's harems and even deny the marital relationship. Adultery, incest, murder and jealousy punctuate other accounts of family life.

The good news is that God still works in families, even rotten ones. God is still the God of Abraham and Isaac and Jacob. Again and again the Bible promises grace to the children and children's children of those who love and trust God; and repeatedly special mercy is shown to families, whether those of Noah or Rahab or the Philippian jailer. The "begats" represent believing folk who struggled to impart their faith to their children as they ate simple meals and walked along the roads or told them bedtime stories.

The faith of parents still ignites the faith of children. It is not automatic or without struggle, but home-grown faith is still contagious. The promise of salvation is still there for those who will believe and also for their children (Acts 2:39).

Saving a Life Versus Saving a Marriage

A seminarian from Asia married a fellow student from the same nation. The abuse began even before the honeymoon was over. Worried for her safety, the young woman reported her fears to administrators of the seminary. She was told that she must endure the mistreatment as a good Christian wife and that God would bring good out of it.

> Jesus said, "There is no one who has left house or wife or brothers or parents or children, for the sake of the kingdom of God, who will not get back very much more in this age, and in the age to come eternal life." (Lk 18:29-30)

Unable to study in her own apartment, she resorted to the cafeteria in order to prepare for an examination. Suddenly the violent husband burst into the dining hall and inflicted considerable damage before other students could restrain him. The woman, along with her husband, was then dismissed from the seminary so that the community would not be further endangered.

At last she was told that concerns for her own safety made a separation advisable. The administration, in a desire to be faithful to Scripture, had come to see that altered priorities were called for.[3]

It is critically important to think biblically about the family. While the family has great importance in Scripture, it is not accorded ultimate status. Jesus indicated that there were other priorities, higher than those of family. His followers must love him far more than they do their own father, mother, spouse, children, brothers or sisters—even more than their own life (Lk 14:26).

His disciples had left their families to follow the Master's call (Mt 4:21-22; Lk 5:11; 18:28). These separations were temporary but nevertheless real. Like the brothers of Jesus, Peter was later to engage in missionary travels with his wife (1 Cor 9:5), but his remark that "we have left all" (Lk 18:28 NIV) indicates that husbands and wives were not always together during our Lord's earthly ministry. Jesus acknowledged that the sacrifice had been made and pointed to a necessity higher than family togetherness.

Jesus also declared that his mission might drive families apart rather than bringing them together (Mt 10:35-37; Lk 12:51-53) and that loyalty to him must supersede family loyalty (Mt 8:21-22; Lk 9:59-62). He himself was homeless (Mt 8:20; Lk 9:58), and relationships with his family were sometimes strained. Some of the interchanges between Jesus and his mother are not altogether harmonious, and he recognized a kinship deeper than the biological one with those who heard the word of God and did it (Mt 12:46-50; Mk 3:31-35; Lk 8:19-21). His family understood him so little that at one point they came to take him away, having concluded that he was "out of his mind" (Mk 3:21).

Later his earthly siblings would become committed leaders in the church who shared important insights with their brothers and sisters in Christ, as the epistles of James and Jude attest. James, the brother of our Lord according to flesh, was a pillar in the church at Jerusalem and a major influence in decision-making at critical junctures in the process of world evangelization (Acts 15:13-21; 21:18-25; Gal 1:18-19; 2:9).

Even in the Holy Family, solidarity did not come easily or without pain. It is not lack of faith to admit that there are difficulties within our families. Is it possible that promoting an unrealistic view of family life can actually compound the problem? Consider how a well-known Christian psychologist characterized an interesting attitude displayed by some of his clients: "We're *going* to have a perfect Christian marriage even if I have to *beat* you to get it!"[4]

A survey by George Barna's organization reveals that born-again Christians divorce at a higher rate (27 percent) than those who are not born again (24 percent). Among Christian denominations, Baptists had the highest rate (29 percent), while those belonging to nondenominational Protestant churches were even more likely to have experienced a divorce (34 percent). Likewise the Jewish faith community, which puts great emphasis on marriage and family, has a high divorce rate (30 percent). Among Christian groups, Catholics and Lutherans, with their emphasis on pastoral counseling, had the lowest rates (Barna 1999).

Glorifying marriage and prescribing rigid roles do not lead to healthy relationships. Rather, a concern for hurting families is more likely to lead to marriages that can be made whole. Within our churches there must be freedom to acknowledge problems and to seek the support of fellow Christians.

When the silence is broken, God's people can address the problem. Energies can be directed to healing instead of hiding. The biblical pattern is not to conceal abuse but to bring it to light and seek solutions. Let us confess that we are the imperfect and sinful people of God. We cannot be a forgiven people until we have confessed our failures and sought restitution and healing. It's messy and costly and embarrassing. But God can work when there is honesty. Separation is not necessarily failure. It may be the path to something far better! God's purposes for the family are higher than ours.

Biblical Metaphors of Marriage

We are fond of saying that marriage is a beautiful metaphor of God's love for his people. We must, in the first instance, understand that a metaphor is a word picture that helps us comprehend what a speaker is trying to convey. If a young woman is told that her cheeks are roses, we understand that her cheeks do not actually have all the qualities of roses. They do not have thorns, are not rooted in dirt and will not attract bees, wither or produce rosehips. Certainly we would not want to imply that a lovely young woman's cheeks were like roses in having a propensity to wither rapidly, to be subject to rot and to thrive on manure. It is important to know where the likeness begins and ends. In fact, there is only one quality that cheeks and roses share—a beautiful color. Even the fragrance is not the same, unless it is achieved with the help of a perfume bottle.

When the Bible speaks of God's marriage to Israel or of the church as the bride of Christ, the concept is a metaphor to help us understand the covenant relationship. What should be the closest and most meaningful human bond is selected to portray divine love. This does not mean that earthly marriage necessarily partakes of heavenly aspects but rather that what is potentially best in human experience is being used to give some understanding of a far more profound reality. The metaphor is intended to convey the tenderness and enduring fidelity of God, the lengths to which God will go to ensure the safety of his beloved.

Marriage as the most intimate of human ties is indeed used as a metaphor, but it is surely not an exemplar. We cannot possibly say that an abusive marriage is a picture of Christ's love for the church. Rather, Christ's love is an exemplar for what earthly marriage should be. The wedding of Christ to his bride, the church, lies in the future. In the meantime the heavenly bridegroom is assisting the bride to be fully developed spiritually, socially and morally. Both parties look forward to a joyous union.

A picture of a failed marriage. The biblical image of God's marriage to Israel is developed not at Sinai where the covenant is made—"I will be your God and you shall be my people" (see Ex 19:1-8)—but after Israel has broken faith with God. When there is no longer faithfulness to the one true God, we find the metaphor of the betrayed husband. He has given all, and the faithless wife has betrayed him.

Actually, the concept is first introduced as a metaphor for an extremely bad marriage. Israel is the flagrantly unfaithful wife and God the heartbroken husband. Isaiah, Jeremiah, Ezekiel and Hosea all represent the covenant relationship of God and his people in terms of a destroyed marriage.

The theme is introduced by Hosea, who lived in the northern kingdom and prophesied in the last days before it fell to Assyria. His was the task of revealing the apostasy of Israel and calling the nation to repentance. God commands Hosea to act out a parable symbolically. He is to take Gomer, a prostitute, as his wife. After she bears three children, her conduct is so wanton that Hosea divorces her. She is set free to pursue her many lovers and suffer the consequences of her behavior. As the marriage has been broken, so has Israel's covenant with God been broken. "You are not my people and I am not your God" (Hos 1:9). God declares, "She is not my wife, and I am not her husband" (2:2). How poignant is the anguish that Hosea expresses, on behalf both of God and of himself!

Israel too has been adulterous, going after other gods, even though she had promised to be true to the Lord. Gone is the covenant that

bound the Israelite people and the abundance and fertility with which
God had blessed them. The separation is bitter for both parties. God
mourns for his people, and Israel will at last realize that God's kindness and mercy are far better than the treachery of her paramours
(Hos 2:7). Ultimately there would be reconciliation, but not until
Israel has known the bitterness of alienation and divorce from the
source of all true good.

Isaiah, Hosea's contemporary, takes up the theme as he addresses
the sins of the southern kingdom. Judah too has been an unfaithful
wife (Is 54:4-6) who has been cast out and will not repent. God has
divorced her because the marriage is now meaningless, devoid of trust
or commitment (50:1). Both the anger and anguish of God are appar-
ent; even the heart of God can be broken.

Yahweh is pictured here not only as husband but also as creator of
a moral universe. In that world God has given human beings freedom
of will. They have liberty to choose their actions but cannot control
the consequences of their choices. Decisions opposed to the will of
God lead to disaster. God is patient and forgiving, but ultimately there
is a price that must be paid for violation of spiritual, ethical and moral
codes.

The picture painted by Jeremiah is even more bleak. Both Judah
and Israel have given themselves to others and must pay the price of
their adultery. Israel has gone into exile with a decree of divorce, yet
Judah continues to play the harlot (Jer 3:1-3, 6-10). It is hard for us
to imagine the degree of apostasy that had been reached. Both the
biblical account and archaeological evidence demonstrate quite
explicitly that the Israelites had adopted the cult and culture of the
neighboring peoples. They practiced every abomination that had been
forbidden them.

God as wronged husband. Such a travesty of marriage could not be
preserved. Yahweh, the wronged husband, ultimately severs the covenant that Israel has breached and institutes a divorce. "What right has
my beloved in my house, when she has done vile deeds?" (Jer 11:15).
"I had sent her away with a decree of divorce. . . . As a faithless wife
leaves her husband, so you have been faithless to me, O house of
Israel" (Jer 3:8, 20).

The most shocking metaphors of broken marriage are to be found in the prophecies of Ezekiel (chapters 16 and 23). In some ways his rendering is the most tender. God finds Jerusalem as an abandoned newborn girl. He takes her up, cleans off the blood of childbirth and tenderly nurtures her. In time she grows up to be a beautiful young woman whom God adorns and cherishes. But Jerusalem turns wanton, forgetting all the kindness that her husband has shown, all the blessings he has heaped on her. She turns instead to heathen lovers preoccupied with luxury and fertility. She is enamored of their opulent lifestyle, their gaudy trappings, their phallic art (23:14, 20). Her lewd behavior is spelled out in detail. At last God declares: "When she carried on her whorings so openly and flaunted her nakedness, I turned in disgust from her, as I had turned from her sister" (23:18).

Yahweh spells out in detail the behavior and infidelity of the one to whom he swore constant love. That love has been rejected and denigrated. Despite his longsuffering, God has not been blind. His patience has ultimately encouraged Judah in her misconduct. The righteousness of his character demands a severance of this farcical relationship.

> Whom did you dread and fear
> so that you lied,
> and did not remember me
> or give me a thought?
> Have I not kept silent and closed my eyes,
> and so you do not fear me? (Is 57:11)

God will not be an enabler. The covenant has been flagrantly broken, and his continued provision for Israel only perpetuates her infidelity.

There are limits to what should be endured in a marriage, whether from infidelity or from other forms of abuse. The heavenly husband is justifiably angry, and he vehemently expresses his anger, insisting on a separation. In the end the time apart will be curative, but not until considerable pain has been endured and well-needed lessons have been learned. During the period of separation the errant wife will discover that her lovers are abusive and destructive. Those by whom she had expected to be enhanced have demeaned and despoiled her.

An aspect often disregarded is Yahweh's respect for Israel and for her own choices, though they are bad ones. The texts reflect God's anger but also a sorrowful acceptance of Israel's rejection of him. Divine action does not force God on anyone. In the moral universe God has created, people must face the consequences of their wrong choices. Although he does not actively bring about the evil, the heavenly husband will no longer shield the errant wife from the bitter products of her own folly.

The forces that swing into effect against Israel are those of her own choosing. Former lovers prove treacherous when they are no longer restrained. God is not a vengeful husband inflicting malicious abuse on a wayward wife but rather a righteous judge who long ago established righteous decrees.

> Your tormentors . . . have said to you,
>> "Bow down, that we may walk on you";
> and you have made your back like the ground
>> and like the street for them to walk on. (Is 51:23)

She has made herself a doormat. Those by whom she had expected to be enhanced have instead demeaned and despoiled her. They, not Yahweh, have abused her. The chastisement she receives is what she herself has sought.

Some women scholars perceive Yahweh as an abusive husband, but it may be more accurate to say that God withdraws the privileges of a wife. Israel had been brought to birth, raised and adorned by her loving bridegroom, but now her ornaments are no longer hers to wear. Marital status is no longer hers, nor protection from the depredations of other cultures and nations. In a world of free choices, evil lurks where one might not expect it.

> Your ways and your doings
>> have brought this upon you.
> This is your doom; how bitter it is!
>> It has reached your very heart. (Jer 4:18; compare 2:17)

The daughter of Zion abused. In this context Jeremiah depicts God's estranged people as a woman at the mercy of her former lovers. Although she had been enamored of them, now they batter her unmercifully. The lovers whom she had chosen are false. Here we find a remarkable perception of the plight of the abused woman

> What are you doing, O devastated one?
>> Why dress yourself in scarlet
>> and put on jewels of gold?
> Why shade your eyes with paint?
>> You adorn yourself in vain.
> Your lovers despise you;
>> they seek your life.
> I hear a cry as of a woman in labor,
>> a groan as of one bearing the first child—
> the cry of the Daughter of Zion gasping for breath,
>> stretching out her hands and saying,
>> "Alas! I am fainting;
>> my life is given over to murderers." (Jer 4:30-31 NIV)

Men who abuse women will find themselves likened in the Bible not to God the tender lover but to the heathen nations that despoil Israel.

But where is there help for the abused woman? Jeremiah expresses enormous compassion as he raises troubling questions:

> Hark, the cry of the daughter of my people
>> from the length and breadth of the land
> "Is the LORD not in Zion?
>> "Is her king not in her?"...
>
> For the wound of the daughter of my people is my heart wounded,
>> I mourn, and dismay has taken hold on me.
>
> Is there no balm in Gilead?
>> Is there no physician there?
> Why then has the health of the daughter of my people
>> not been restored?
> O that my head were waters,
>> and my eyes a fountain of tears,
> that I might weep day and night
>> for the slain of the daughter of my people! (Jer 8:19, 21—9:1 RSV)

Jeremiah's poignant description leaves us with no doubt that God

empathizes with those who have suffered abuse, even if their judgment has not always been good. At last the erring wife says to herself
that it was better when she was with her true husband (see Hos 2:7).
She decides to flee her abusive lovers, to seek forgiveness and the
reestablishment of the marriage.

God as reconciling husband. There must of necessity be a separation, but amid the tragedy of a dissolved marriage, God gives promise
of renewal and reconciliation. Isaiah in particular spells out the tender
reconciling love of the heavenly husband:

> For the LORD has called you
>   like a wife forsaken and grieved in spirit,
> like the wife of a man's youth when she is cast off,
>   says your God.
> For a brief moment I abandoned you,
>   but with great compassion I will gather you. (Is 54:6-7)

The wife who was bruised and abused by her lovers is now promised
a future in which she shall have a home free of violence.

Viable Conclusions from the Biblical Metaphor

What conclusions may we draw from this tragic metaphor that still
promises a happy ending? How can we apply this material to the current problem of domestic abuse? In the biblical parable the wife is
clearly the abuser of the marriage, although she suffers cruelly herself.

If we seek to draw a paradigm from the metaphor of God's marriage to Israel, then we must be mindful of its implications. First we
must note that God is not portrayed as vindictive abuser but as righteous spouse who refuses to allow his wife's flagrantly wanton conduct to continue indefinitely. Even in this picture of marriage where
one spouse is our loving God, there are limits. There must be a time of
separation.

And even after repentance the reconciliation is not instantaneous.
Like Gomer, Judah must be given the opportunity to prove herself.
This can come, however, only after repentance and a period of prov-
ing that it is genuine (Hos 3:3). In the case of Israel, the period of
waiting is a long one (vv. 4-5).

If God can institute a protracted time of waiting for Israel's change of heart (Is 54:6-7), should not victims of abuse wait for evidence of a truly changed heart on the part of the abuser? Even God does not shield the offender from the consequences of her own mistakes. We must be careful not to deprive perpetrators of the opportunity to grow through reaping the harvest of what they have sown.

We may learn most, however, from the wonderful promises of domestic tranquillity and safety as God envisions a joyous reunion: "My people will abide in a peaceful habitation, / in secure dwellings, and in quiet resting places" (Is 32:18). If we are to use God's love for Israel as a paradigm for the marriage of believers, we must include this fundamental objective of peace and safety for all within the household. Indeed, the prophetic promises of a wonderful reconciliation are put in the future. Israel has been the offender, but God takes the lead in fashioning a renewed marriage covenant. The picture of reconciliation is a beautiful one that can well be a model of Christian family life (Is 54:6-7). The wife who was

> The days are surely coming, says the LORD, when I will make a new covenant with the house of Israel and the house of Judah. It will not be like the covenant that I made with their ancestors when I took them by the hand to bring them out of the land of Egypt—a covenant that they broke, though I was their husband, says the LORD. (Jer 31:31-32)

bruised and abused by her lovers is now promised a home free of violence: "I have sworn that I will not be angry with you / and will not rebuke you" (v. 9).

A feature of many abusive marriages is the deliberate humiliation of one spouse. Self-image is destroyed as the individual is made to feel inadequate. But God's pattern is one of empowerment and affirmation, not disgrace and defamation: "Do not fear, for you will not be ashamed; / do not be discouraged, for you will not suffer disgrace" (v. 4). Recrimination is not part of God's reconciliation package; there will be no inducement of guilt or shame, no slurs on her past, no innuendo or unkind allusions.

> For the mountains may depart
>   and the hills be removed,

but my steadfast love shall not depart from you,
and my covenant of peace shall not be removed,
says the LORD, who has compassion on you. (v. 10)

In volatile marriages there often is a cycle of abuse. An incidence of violence or intense mistreatment is followed by a period of contrition, with promises that the behavior will not be repeated. Gradually the tension builds to another eruption of destructive behavior. Extravagant promises are made, only to be broken. With God it is not so. His promises are eternal, his love unfailing. There is no volatility with God, only the steadfastness of kind treatment.

In many instances children who see violence in the home later perpetuate violence in their own families. But God's promises include peace and instruction in righteousness for children (v. 13). They will learn new patterns of family life, of holiness, faith and love.

So Zion will find a new basis for her existence. Her life will be ruled not by fear and oppression but by righteousness and peace (v. 14). She is promised growth and stability, a rediscovery of her own integrity within the forgiveness and acceptance of her heavenly husband. Home life will be characterized by peace rather than strife; the wife will be secure against all violence:

If anyone stirs up strife,
it is not from me;
whoever stirs up strife with you
shall fall because of you. . . .
No weapon that is fashioned against you shall prosper
and you shall confute every tongue that rises against you in
judgment. (vv. 15, 17)

Verbal abuse will be prohibited, as will word twisting, ridicule and insult. More than this, the wife is promised empowerment to rise to her own defense—to become a full person in her own right. She has been delivered from physical, mental and sexual abuse, and brought to a place of safety and assurance.

9

Repentance
& Forgiveness

H e broke my arm, and then I had to get right back into bed with him," grieved a woman whose faith community had forced her into a premature reconciliation with her husband.[1] Too often Christians demand that others forgive immediately, before it is appropriate or advisable, before there can be adequate contrition, reflection or amelioration.

Forgiveness: A Long Road
Although the Bible does exhort us to forgive, it does not insist on our returning to the circumstances that occasioned an offense in the first place. Forgiveness does not necessarily imply reconciliation. In the case of domestic violence, to continue on as before may throw open the door to continued abuse. The perpetrator may see that the consequences of his or her misbehavior were relatively light. A period of time in which to prove himself is likely to be more curative of both soul and emotions. A time of separation from his family is more likely

to be conducive of willingness to change and take whatever steps are necessary to bring about that change. The abuser may become willing to accept counseling, to put himself under the care of an accountability group, to join a batterers' group. Such a process does not bring an automatic resolution to the difficulty that many Christians would like to see, but we are instructed to "let endurance have its full effect" (Jas 1:4).

All of us have wronged others and been wronged ourselves; and all of us understand the need for healing in such situations. But the healing must be done in a careful and prayerful process as the Holy Spirit gives enablement. The first step is simply to acknowledge to oneself that there has indeed been a hurt. If we are the offender, then we must repent and seek to make matters right with the one whom we have harmed. If we ourselves have been hurt, then we must first admit that the offense did indeed occur. If we deny the reality of what has happened, the wound will only fester. The apostle Paul wrote, "Alexander the coppersmith did me much harm" (2 Tim 4:14).

In the healing process, we need to be clear-sighted enough to understand the responsibility of the person who wronged us. If we are partially at fault, that must be acknowledged; but ultimately we must also understand what is *not* our fault and *not* our responsibility. If we are confused about responsibility, we will probably continue to harbor vengeful feelings. It was helpful to Paul to be clear about Alexander's role in what had happened to him. He appears to write without rancor, simply stating a fact that might enable someone else to steer clear of dangerous waters.

Paul does not end with identifying the person who wronged him but with the conviction that "the Lord will pay him back for his deeds" (2 Tim 4:14). The Bible discourages us from "getting even"; instead it gives numerous promises that God will take care of vengeance (Lev 19:18; Deut 32:35; Prov 24:12; Rom 12:17-21; 1 Thess 5:15; Heb 10:30). In this matter we may experience a real struggle of faith, but we may safely leave the matter in God's hands. Perhaps this explains why many of the psalms are quite angry and why hostilities toward one's enemies are fully expressed. We need to let God know just how we feel. Then it is God's job to bring justice and transformation to the troubled situation.

We need also to understand that the ability to forgive comes from God in a long-range work of grace. This may be embarrassing to a faith community seeking quick fixes, but the victim needs time to experience this work of grace on a timetable that is not ours to determine. Forgiveness was purchased at the cost of God's only Son, and that gift can bring us through our own struggles to forgive.

Aphiēmi, the Greek word for "forgive," means to put something away, set it free, as well as to put one thing aside in order to move on to something else. Forgiveness is essentially a putting away of our anger toward another, putting it aside so that it no longer controls our lives. Only by doing so can we be free to move on to something better. We are told to "leave room for God's wrath" (Rom 12:19 NIV) just as we are exhorted to be angry but not to sin (Eph 4:26; cf. Ps 4:4; Jas 1:19-20). *Apolyō,* another word for forgiving, has as well the idea of loosing or freeing ourselves from anger and resentment toward another.

Instead of holding something against another, we will be able to release it and thereby to be free of the grip that hatred, resentment and vindictiveness have had on us. Breaking free can be a long and difficult process. We cannot go ahead as though nothing has happened. We need the freedom to acknowledge the harm that has been done and to assess the damage wreaked in our own lives and the lives of those we love. It is good to be able to share this with a trusted confidant. Better yet is to open up one's heart to God.

We cannot rid ourselves of anger until we have examined the cause. The so-called imprecatory psalms can be exceedingly useful here. The psalmist pours out his pain, rage and sense of injury. Negative feelings that we would be ashamed to air in God's presence are exposed in full detail. Like the psalmist, we need the opportunity to spread out the shame, hurt, distress and bewilderment we have experienced. Within the psalms an abused woman will find many expressions of her own feelings and circumstances. The psalms were both the hymnbook and the prayerbook of ancient Israel, and they have been so used by God's people ever since. If they can express our sentiments in times of trouble, they can also guide us to look at the King of

Glory who leads us to new confidence and joy.

The Need for Separation

Although we can by God's grace ultimately give up deep grudges against an abusive spouse, there may well need to be a time of moving apart. When Jacob and Esau were at last reconciled, they still found it best to live apart (Gen 33:1-17). Paul separated from Barnabas after they quarreled over the defection of Mark (Acts 15:36-39; cf. Gal 2:13). There was later a reconciliation even though they no longer traveled together (Col 4:10; 2 Tim 4:11). Peter and Paul had a sharp disagreement (Gal 2:11-14) that was later resolved with the help of the Jerusalem Council as the boundaries of their individual ministries were defined (Gal 2:1-10). Though they maintained subsequent distance from each other, the writings of both apostles show evidence of profound respect and mutual cooperation (1 Cor 1:12; 3:22; Gal 2:7-8; 2 Pet 3:15-16).

The victim of domestic abuse will be better able to come to a point of forgiveness if she does not immediately return to the situation that triggered the abuse in the first place. Forgiveness does not mean going on as though nothing ever

---

Marie Fortune (1998) lists helpful guidelines for forgiveness:

What Forgiveness Is Not
1. Forgiveness is not condoning or pardoning harmful behavior, which is a sin.
2. Forgiveness is not healing the wound lightly, saying "peace, peace" when there is not peace.
3. Forgiveness is not always possible.
4. Forgiveness is not an expectation of any degree of future relationship with the person who caused the harm.

What Forgiveness Is
1. Forgiveness is letting go so that the immediacy of the painful memories can be put into perspective.
2. Forgiveness is possible in a context of justice-making and the healing presence of the Holy Spirit.
3. Forgiveness is God's gift, for the purpose of healing, to those who have been harmed.
4. Accountability is God's gift to those who have harmed another for the purpose of repentance (read "fundamental change").

happened. Neither God nor human beings can forgive in a vacuum. Repentance calls for a transformed attitude and lifestyle. Before reconciling with his brothers, Joseph engaged in an elaborate stratagem to test the genuineness of their repentance (Gen 42—44). Jesus and his followers called for a repentance that goes far beyond a mere expression of contrition (Mt 3:8; Lk 3:8; 19:8-9; Acts 26:20; Eph 4:28; cf. Is 1:16-17). Whether or not a woman decides to be reunited with her husband, the offender needs enough time to take the steps required for true recovery.

If reconciliation is to occur, the groundwork should be laid carefully. If there is too hasty a reunion, the abuser may conclude that the offense was not actually a serious one because the consequences are so light. The victim needs time to pray and think through many aspects and implications of a reunion. Both parties must carefully consider how to prevent a recurrence of the abuse and victimization. In effecting a reunion, the faith community may be very helpful, though members must be very careful not to rush or force the process. After reconciliation, the church should continue to lend support and step in to help whenever the need arises.

A helpful step for Christian victims (as part of the healing journey) may be to embark on prayers that they will at some point be able to forgive their offenders. Through prayer over time, anger may dissipate and the impact of painful memories can be placed within a broader life narrative. Healing for victims and accountability for offenders are the twin pillars of God's response to abuse, and praying brings about the will of God.

10

Cruel Deceptions & Christian Conceptions

s the prayer meeting convened, I requested prayer for an incarcerated Christian, an evangelical of many years' standing, who had killed his wife and children. A middle-aged man responded, "Be sure not to tell anyone that he was a born-again Christian."

We are bound by a conspiracy of silence!

I have been told of a prominent Christian leader who made three separate attempts to kill his wife. On the third occasion he left her for dead in a wood. Miraculously, she managed to crawl out and get help. Now she was forced to consider seriously God's call on her life. Why had she been given an extension of her life? How could she be a faithful steward of that gift?

When at last the woman filed for divorce, she was bitterly condemned by her church. Her husband was the pastor as well as a professor in a Bible college. The congregation declared that she should never have revealed the abuse but should have kept it hidden. But to have complied with their wishes and continued the secrecy would almost surely have led to her murder.

All of us need to reexamine our attitudes on the issue of silence.

The Challenge of Interpretation

As our introductory chapters have demonstrated, one-quarter of the world's women, whether Christian or non-Christian, are victims of domestic abuse and violence. Some societies may show a higher rate of abuse than others, but few show minimal abuse. Careful and repeated research demonstrates that domestic violence happens in all cultures, all ages, all races, all socioeconomic groups and all faith communities.

We must be very careful not to send a wrong message. Tragically, it is the attitudes that produce the behavior, and a distorted theology can give warrant to the sin. Abusive conduct is sometimes condoned by the faith community in its desire to justify an active member of the household of faith. The Bible gives no justification for abuse, even when practiced by a prize deacon.

There are many who manufacture a justification, however. When asked why he had beaten his wife, one man replied,

> Rebellious and stubborn, that's what she is. And I believe firmly in the Bible. So I have the means . . . even hitting, I want to do and have done all that I can to make her like other women. You cannot stand the order of creation on its head. Only the man is the Lord of Creation, and he cannot allow himself to be dominated by womenfolk. So hitting has been my way of marking—that I'm a man, a masculine man, no softie of a man, no cushy type. (Lundgren 1994:37)

The problem has arisen in part because of a serious misinterpretation of the Bible. Peter speaks of ignorant and unstable people who distort the Scriptures to their own destruction—and that of their victims (2 Pet 3:16). The entrance of God's Word brings light. When we fail to proclaim the teaching of Scripture on the issue, we are not adequately using the Word for doctrine, for reproof, for correction and for instruction in righteousness. If we do not declare the biblical condemnation of domestic violence, we restrict God's power in the lives of believers. All too often our denial and minimization have served to cloak the sin.

The error of denial. It is exceedingly hard for us to believe or admit that domestic violence does exist in Christian homes. Because of this, there are few evangelical resources available to help the offender, the victim, the children and the congregation. All too often Christian leaders have maintained that the problem of domestic violence is greatly exaggerated and does not have any particular relevance to born-again believers.

> Is it not [God's command] to share your
>   bread with the hungry,
>   and bring the homeless poor into
>   your house;
> when you see the naked, to cover them,
>   and not to hide yourself from your
>   own kin? . . .
> If you remove the yoke from among
>   you,
>   the pointing of the finger, the
>   speaking of evil,
> if you offer your food to the hungry
>   and satisfy the needs of the afflicted,
> then your light shall rise in the
>   darkness
>   and your gloom be like the noonday.
> (Is 58:7, 9-10)

This book is intended to open the eyes of God's people to the sad reality of what is happening in Christian homes. Israel's prophets were called to denounce evil and call for an end to oppression. The Word of God was applied to the problem perceived and proclaimed by the prophets. Before there could be social justice, there needed to be an understanding of abuse. Jesus said, "You will know the truth, and the truth will make you free" (Jn 8:32). It is only as we acknowledge the sad facts that we can be God's servants in addressing this great evil.

The error of concealment, secrecy and silence. Secrecy is not the path that the Scriptures teach. Moses declares, "Be sure your sin will find you out" (Num 32:23). Jesus maintains that what has been hidden will be revealed upon the housetops (Mt 10:26; Mk 4:22; Lk 8:17; 12:2-3). The biblical paradigm is not to conceal abuse but to deal with it. Until we come to this realization, we can help neither our fellow Christians nor those outside of Christ.

The difficulty arises not because we wish to ignore evil but because we do not know how to deal with domestic abuse biblically. Often we find it easier to deny, ignore, silence or minimize than to address the reality. We fear that to reveal the problem would destroy our testimony to the world. The truth is that we harm our testimony far more by refusing to address the sin that is so prevalent in our midst.

The error of presuming on God's protection. Basing their belief on 1 Peter 3:6, some believers have declared that a woman should not be afraid to return to a dangerous situation, since God will protect her. But Jesus denounced the immorality of deliberately placing oneself in a life-threatening situation. When challenged by Satan to hurl himself from the temple pinnacle so that angels might bear him up, he declared, "Do not put the Lord your God to the test" (Mt 4:7).

There is a time for self-sacrifice—for the sake of the gospel, to save the life of another, to remain faithful to Christ—but surely not to enable the misbehavior of another. The seventh commandment implies that believers should take all possible steps to prevent murder rather than to implement it.

The error of discouraging a victim from finding shelter. Some godly folk do not like to see husband and wife separated, even when there is a danger that one might kill or permanently maim the other. Yet the Bible speaks with approbation of a number of flights to safety (Gen 13:7-11; 14:8-16; 21:9-21; 25:8-9; 27:41-45; 32:1—33:16; 45:4-15, Josh 2:15; 1 Sam 19:11-12; Acts 9:23-25; 2 Cor 2:32-33), and sometimes separation is a means of achieving peace (Gen 13:7-11; 14:8-16; 21:9-21; 25:8-9; 27:41-45; 32:1—33:16; 45:4-15; Acts 15:36-41).

While Christians may in some circumstances risk their lives for the sake of the gospel (Rom 16:3-4), they should not be exhorted to enter or return to life-threatening situations that might be avoided (Mt 4:5-7; Acts 9:23-24; 12:17; 14:19-20; 17:5-10; 19:29-31; 23:10, 12-24). Jesus himself avoided several highly dangerous situations (Lk 4:28-30; Jn 8:59; 10:39).

The error of boycotting available resources. The good news is that there are many ways the people of God can be instruments of God's healing. There are many courses of action that can be put in place within a congregation, and there are community resources that can be used in partnership with the church's program. The Bible tells us to follow after the things that make for peace (Rom 14:19) and to actively pursue peace (Ps 34:14; 2 Tim 2:22; Heb 12:14). The apostle

Paul understood that sometimes marital separation is necessary in order to achieve peace (1 Cor 7:15). Separation can also bring safety. But where is safety to be found?

In a volatile situation, a community resource may well be an excellent way to ensure safety for everyone. Establishing a secure shelter requires a great deal of time, money and expertise. It is a wonderful thing for a church to set up its own facility for abused women and children, but the congregation must understand the demands that will be made on it. Such an operation is dangerous because lives are at stake.

> O that I had in the desert
>   a traveler's lodging place,
> that I might leave my people
>   and go away from them! . . .
> for they proceed from evil to
>   evil. . . .
> Oppression upon oppression,
>   deceit upon deceit! . . .
> They all speak friendly words
>   to their neighbors,
> but inwardly are planning to
>   lay an ambush. (Jer 9:2-
> 3, 6, 8)

Even Christians sometimes become killers of their families. This means that shelter workers too are at risk and that security must become a major concern. Staffing is a special challenge, because careful preparation is necessary to train workers so that they can deal with highly sensitive issues. Again, the most competent and well-trained workers may be found within the community resource system. They may be best able to help with emergency counseling, procuring a restraining order, making provision for the children, providing transportation to work and school, and attending to the many other arrangements necessary for a family in distress.

Many shelters seek some measure of protection by keeping the location a secret. The location must not be divulged. Sometimes, in the hope of effecting a reconciliation, well-meaning Christians reveal a shelter's whereabouts to an abusive spouse. Thereby they place all the residents and staff in danger.

God's provision of a hiding place is a prominent theme in the Bible (Ps 32:7; 55:8; 119:114). Isaiah promises that God will equip the righteous to be a refuge.

> Each will be like a hiding place from the wind,
>   a covert from the tempest,
> like streams of water in a dry place,

like the shade of a great rock in a weary land. (Is 32:2)

The role of providing refuge is often best performed in cooperation with existing local facilities. There are many biblical precedents. The Hebrew spies did not hesitate to avail themselves of Rahab's rope to escape from Jericho (Josh 2:15), nor Jacob and his family to partake of Egypt's grain during a time of famine (Gen 47:1-12). In order to escape the murderous madness of Saul, David fled to the land of the Philistines (1 Sam 27:1-7); previously he had found safety for his parents with the king of Moab (1 Sam 22:2-4). Elijah found safety outside the community of faith in the home of a Phoenician widow (1 Kings 17:8-24; Lk 4:25-26).

A local shelter may well be the best resource, and there is good biblical warrant for using such a facility to help a member of the household of faith. If we are concerned that the victim may not receive positive messages about the church, then we need to carry the message of God's care and concern to the shelter. We can model Christ's compassion to those both inside and outside the fold.

11

Good News for
& About Abusers

Abusers are often frightened, insecure people who need the
grace of God in their lives. Surprisingly, many have a great
fear that their spouses will leave them, and they seek to prevent this abandonment by the various kinds of control that they exert.
And so the cycle of misery is perpetuated. Often "tough love" is the best
way to bring them to transformed attitudes.

An evangelical woman who runs several court-mandated batterers
groups for a sheriff's office finds that born-again Christians are the
persons who most often ask to be excused from a group.[1] Somehow
they feel that they are above associating with ordinary sinners. Sometimes a pastor will try to convince a judge that he can counsel a perpetrator on a one-on-one basis. But group therapy has been shown to be
very effective for batterers. It is important to understand that abuse
involves sinful conduct and that offenders should receive no special
leniency. The Bible speaks of appropriate judgment! Christians
should not try to help the perpetrator escape the consequences of the

behavior. This is no kindness to anyone.

Don't Give Up on God

All parties should understand that it is exceedingly difficult for abusers to alter their patterns of behavior. The victim should not entertain false hopes; the church should not assume that change is being effected. In fact most abusers do not change, even though they may profess repentance and promise never to repeat their behavior. We knew of one man who deceived two different accountability groups to which he was supposedly answering.[2] He had a very hard time changing!

But God's power is still adequate to bring about radically altered conduct. The fanatic Saul who murdered Christians became the apostle Paul, the bearer of the gospel of life. While "breathing out threatenings and slaughter" he was stopped short by a direct intervention of the risen Christ, and from that time forth he was never the same.

David, livid with anger, was deflected from murderous intentions against an entire family by a wise and gracious intervention. He himself had been living a precarious existence, hunted and hounded by paranoid King Saul, who sought his life. David had retreated to a cave in the wilderness, where he was joined by others who had fled Saul's regime (1 Sam 22:1-2). In that wild territory David and his men provided local farmers with protection from marauders. In return he expected compensation. When David's emissaries arrived to collect payment, one farmer, Nabal (Hebrew for "churl"), refused to supply any sort of remuneration and quite gratuitously insulted David's parentage.

The hot-tempered exile was not prepared to accept this incivility, which he rightly perceived as an affront both to the conscientious efforts of his men and to himself personally. Although he had refrained from slaying Saul when he had opportunity, his present rage placed him in a very different mood. He gathered a band of followers and started off with the explicit purpose of slaughtering every male in Nabal's household. In the meantime Abigail, the churl's wise and judicious wife, learned of the incident and realized that reparations must be made in haste. She loaded pack mules with bread, wine, cheese, meat and other goods and hurried up the hill with her retinue.

So it was that the war party headed down the hill, intent on slaughter, was met by the peace party on its way up, intent on reconciliation. The wise woman bowed to David and offered her apologies, but more important, she reminded him of God's purpose. He had been anointed king of Israel, and the murders that he intended would always be a blot on one who was to be raised up by God as defender of the Israelite people.

The would-be murderer perceived that he had been delivered from the unrighteous action he had planned. It behooved him not only to care for sheep but also to care for people, even recalcitrant ones. David responded gratefully to Abigail:

> Blessed be the LORD, the God of Israel, who sent you to meet me today! Blessed be your good sense, and blessed be you, who have kept me today from bloodguilt and from avenging myself by my own hand! For as surely as the LORD the God of Israel lives, who has restrained me from hurting you, unless you had hurried and come to meet me, truly by morning there would not have been left to Nabal so much as one male." (1 Sam 25:32-35)

Yes, by God's power and the faithful witness of godly people, the violent can become peaceful.

Consistent with this pattern is the story of David's general Joab, who laid siege to a city without following the biblical command that first there must be communication and a definition of the issues (Deut 20:10). He commanded a ramp to be built in order to scale the city's fortifications. The entire population was endangered, yet the people inside did not know why they were being attacked.

A wise woman saw the dire straits to which her city had been reduced, and she had the moral courage to mount the city wall and demand a hearing with Joab. She reminded him that she was obeying the dictates of God and inquired why he was threatening the city and its people with extermination. The loss, she pointed out, would be great to the entire nation. This little city of Abel Beth Maacah was famed for the wise counsel that its citizens dispensed to people who came from all over Israel seeking advice. She asked, "Why will you swallow up the heritage of the LORD?"

Realizing the moral implications, Joab quickly retrenched his position: "Far be it from me, far be it, that I should swallow up or destroy!" For the first time he explained the problem: a rebel named Sheba, intent on forcible overthrow of David's government, had taken refuge in the city and must be captured. The woman effected a wise resolution: the wise city would deal with the offender itself. This they did with directness and dispatch. Joab lifted the siege and went home in peace (2 Sam 20:1-22).

The valiant Queen Esther risked her very life to intervene for the endangered Jewish people. Only then did her husband realize the vicious plan for their extermination to which he had unwittingly given his consent.

Let us not forget that confronting people on moral grounds can make a difference. We can be faithful witnesses of what the Scriptures have to tell us. While every effort must be made to keep victims safe, we must never underestimate the power of the Holy Spirit in the lives of sinful people.

The Command for Zero Tolerance

"Put away violence and oppression, and do what is just and right," commands Ezekiel (45:9). God's people are expected to repudiate the ways and companionship of the violent. The righteous avoid the ways of the violent (Ps 17:4). The writer of Proverbs cautions, "Do not envy the wicked, nor desire to be with them; for their minds devise violence, and their lips talk of mischief" (Prov 24:1-2). The same thought is repeated in Proverbs 3:31: "Do not envy the violent and do not choose any of their ways." For other injunctions to avoid the company of the violent, see Proverbs 1:10-16 and 16:29.

The New Testament as well calls for denunciation and intervention in such cases (Mt 18: 15-17; 1 Cor 5:1-6; 1 Thess 5:14; 1 Tim 4:20; Tit 3:2-11; Jas 5:19-20). "Take note of those who do not obey what we say in this letter; have nothing to do with them, so that they may be ashamed. Do not regard them as enemies, but warn them as believers" (2 Thess 3:14-15).

Furthermore, the Pastoral Epistles twice warn not to put a violent person into a position of church leadership (1 Tim 3:3; Tit 1:7). The

Greek noun *plēktēs* means literally one who beats or batters. Though translated "violent" in many of our modern translations, the King James Version very accurately renders the term "striker." Abusing one's family is an automatic disqualification for appointive leadership in the church.

Corrective Measures

But the Scriptures repeatedly tell us that if a brother or sister is overtaken in a fault, it is the duty of the church to lead the offender back into paths of righteousness. Frequently church leaders are terribly embarrassed and uncomfortable at the thought of having to address an offender. More often than not, no direct dialogue ever takes place, and the perpetrator assumes that the problem is not very serious after all. To pastoral counselors who feel embarrassed, inept or uncomfortable about broaching the subject with the abuser, Carol Adams suggests speaking along these lines:

> The counselor might say: "Speaking about your abuse of your wife is an affirmation of your relationship with God. This naming offers reconnection, reconnecting you with a saving God, and reconnecting yourself with behavior that treats your partner as an equal and worthy of dignity. But now that you have named the behavior, the work can begin. It won't be easy but God will be with you in this work."
> (Adams 1994:45)

> I am on your side as you become a person who does not batter. I am against your battering behavior. I do not believe you should treat your wife as an object that can be battered. But I am in total support of you as you seek to change.
>
> I am calling you to repent and to change. You will probably suffer in the process of change. You cannot rely on old coping mechanisms that include battering. New life is possible, but it requires work. (Adams 1994:92)

At a later stage the batterer—when he is willing to acknowledge his behavior—can be helped to repentance and reconciliation with God.

Firmness on the Road to Restoration

Firmness is more likely to bring transformation than ignoring the problem. Indeed, failing to address the situation may convey to the offender that the sin is not really so bad. The New Testament speaks of the work that may be done in the hearts of errant believers even while they are being disciplined by the church: "You are to hand this man over to Satan for the destruction of the flesh, so that his spirit may be saved in the day of the Lord" (1 Cor 5:5; see also 1 Tim 1:10). The church may mentor, monitor and minister, but there can be no pretending that everything is all right.

Neither can the church accept an abuser's excuses. If the spouse's behavior has been less than perfect, that is still not justification for striking her. There are other ways to resolve differences. Anger is frequently used as justification for battering, but the Scriptures warn us not to sin when we are angry (Eph 4:26).

Mere rebuke is not enough. The community of faith is called to action rather than indifference. It is tempting to say that what goes on in somebody else's home is none of our business; but that is not true in the household of faith. Steps must be taken to ensure that the abuse is stopped. This will require time, effort and endurance from the church.

It is very good if the abuser asks forgiveness and promises never to repeat the offense, and even his tears may be of value. Yet even confession in front of the church body may not produce altered behavior. The perpetrator needs to be helped to hold himself accountable. An accountability group may prove helpful, but offenders sometimes deceive even their accountability group. It is necessary that there be fruits worthy of repentance (Jer 35:15; Mt 3:8; Lk 3:8; Acts 26:20). This means taking whatever steps are necessary so that the abuse is not repeated.

In Massachusetts, Batterers Intervention Programs are certified by the Department of Public Health. In the words of Beth Gerhardt, director of a certified batterers intervention program:

> the course includes eighty hours of group intervention, group methodology that focuses on the batterer taking responsibility for his abuse. . . . Domestic violence is not viewed as just an individual problem, but rather as a societal and human rights issue. The entire community needs to respond to help the victim and hold the batterer accountable. The good news is that these programs believe that the abuser can change!

Gerhardt insists that effective intervention programs have as a goal to teach batterers that abuse is a lose-lose situation for both his partner and himself. "Let endurance have its full effect" (Jas 1:4). When abuse happens in church families, everyone should understand that there cannot be an instantaneous solution. Situations that developed over years cannot be addressed in a day.

It is always easier to look the other way than to demand redress for evil, but to this God has summoned us; and we must shoulder the responsibility for problems that we in part have helped to create. If we have tolerated a shocking situation in our midst, then we must pray, study and act to right the wrong. This book is a call to such prayer, study and action.

12

The Biblical Option
of Divorce

O ften an abuser feels no real need to change because he is convinced that divorce is not an option. He assumes that a good Christian wife is required to remain with him regardless of his treatment of her. Actually, in this way we ignore a major instrument that can be used to correct inappropriate behavior. Divorce is clearly the least desirable option, but sometimes it is a necessary option; and it is indeed a biblical option. The possibility of divorce reinforces the serious nature of the offense and serves as an incentive for changing abusive conduct. An evangelical therapist who operates several groups for batterers reports that men participate not because of a court order but because of their wives' mandate. Failure to attend group meetings will result in divorce.[1]

When God Divorces
When we announce that the Lord hates divorce, we do not add that the same verse declares that God hates violence. Indeed the Malachi

2:16 passage is translated alternatively by the New International Version thus: " 'I hate divorce,' says the LORD God of Israel, 'and I hate a man's covering his wife with violence as well as with his garment,' says the LORD Almighty. So guard yourself in your spirit, and do not break faith."

Why do we not tell victims and abusers that Proverbs 6:17-19 lists seven things that the Lord hates: "haughty eyes, a lying tongue, and hands that shed innocent blood, a heart that devises wicked plans, feet that hurry to run to evil, a lying witness who testifies falsely, and one who sows discord in a family"? Why do we compel a victim to remain in a marriage characterized by these seven evils that the Lord hates? All too often the preservation of marriage has been exalted as the highest good, even when human life is at stake. This is not what the Bible says.

Marriage was given to bind together a man and woman as one flesh in enduring union (Gen 2:24; Eph 5:31). Much in the Bible is said to safeguard the bonds of matrimony (Ex 20:14; Lev 20:10; Deut 5:18; 22:22) and to affirm the strength of permanent marriage (Prov 2:16-17; 5:15-20; 12:4; 18:22). It was the duty of a husband to "bring happiness to his wife" (Deut 23:5). Individual marriages involved private covenants within the larger context of the covenant with Israel.

At Mount Sinai the people had agreed to a covenant by which God would set Israel apart from all the nations of the earth. They were to demonstrate to the rest of humanity what it meant to serve the true and living God. In return, God promised to bless them and to be their God as they were to Yahweh a dedicated people.

According to the covenant between God and Israel, the believing community promised not to give their daughters in marriage to those of alien faith nor to take for their sons wives who did not worship the Lord (Ex 34:16). This was a promise not only to God but to the entire faith community. To embrace those who adored false gods was to vitiate a covenant intended to extend from one generation to another. Those within the covenant community were required to marry a believing spouse and to instruct their children in the ways of the Lord. This knowledge of the true and living God was at the very core of the cohesion and perpetuity of Israel. Faith was passed from one generation to another; the genealogies that seem so boring are in fact a dynamic account of that transmission.

With the giving of the law, however, provision was made for human sin. As there was sacrifice for those who trespassed, so there was also provision for divorce in case of untenable situations (Deut 24:1). A formal document gave termination and clarification to what otherwise might be a confused situation (see Judg 15:1-3).

God's covenant with Israel was likened to a marriage union, one that was betrayed by an idolatrous wife. At three points in Scripture we are told that Yahweh has divorced his people (Is 50:1; 54:6-7; Jer 3:8). Divorce was given not as a desirable option but as the least undesirable one in certain cases. The evangelical church cannot wholly condemn an action adopted by the Lord of heaven and earth in response to willful and persistent human sin.

Divorce and Covenant Restoration

A passage in the Old Testament recounts the writing of a decree of divorce for those who would reestablish a covenant relationship with God. Judah as well as Israel had lapsed into idolatry, but in Babylon there had been a renewed study of the Scriptures and a commitment to the ways of the Word. The dispossessed and chastened people had returned to Palestine to build anew a nation committed to God, but the return had brought for some a transgression of the covenant between God and the people. They had set aside their believing wives to forge more advantageous matches with local landowners' daughters.

It was this practice that Malachi condemned (Mal 2:11-14). Forbidden intermarriage had brought acculturation with the heathen rather than perseverance in God's call to holiness (Ezra 9:1-2; compare Ex 34:15-16; Deut 7:3-4). Just such intermarriage and acculturation had destroyed the identity of the ten northern tribes; now those who remained were exposed to the possibility of the same fate.

Ezra commanded unfaithful Israelites to divorce their mates if they wished to continue as part of the covenant community (Ezra 9:10— 10:11). Unlike Ruth and Rahab, who embraced the faith of Israel, these Gentile wives had rejected the patterns and culture of Judaic lifestyle.

The husbands had invested so little in their home life that half of the children could not even understand the Hebrew language (Neh 13:23-25). Thereby the offspring were denied an understanding of the Scriptures and of God's purposes for their lives, both individually and collectively. These marriages were a violation of the covenant itself (Ezra 9:10-15) and constituted a threat to the continuing faith of Israel.

Even the priests and Levites had forgotten their sacred duty not only to conduct the worship of Israel's God but also to train their children for the holy office (Ezra 10:18-44; Num. 1:53; 3:5—4:49; 8:19). Nehemiah prayed, "Remember them, O my God, because they have defiled the priesthood, the covenant of the priests and the Levites" (Neh 13:29; compare Ezra 9:1). The priests and Levites had a spiritual obligation to the whole of Israel. Only descendants of Aaron might offer incense and conduct the services of worship (Num 16:40; 18:1-7; 2 Chron 26:18). The priesthood was for them a gift (Num 18:7) and a responsibility. A concomitant obligation was instruction in the ways of God (Lev 10:8-11; 2 Chron 15:3; 17:7-9; Ezra 8:25; Neh 8:7-8; Mal 2:7). Theirs as well was the duty of judging disputes and maintaining public health standards in order to ensure the well-being of the community (Lev 13:2—14:56; Deut 17:8-13; 19:17; 21:5; 24:8; 1 Chron 23:3-4; 26:29; 2 Chron 19:8-11; Ezek 44:24). For others to attempt this ministry was considered heinous sacrilege (Num 16:1-40; 2 Chron 26:16-21).

Descendants of Aaron were required to marry women of other priestly families and to train their children from infancy in the traditions of Israel's cult (Lev 21:7, 13-14; Ezek 44:22). Early childhood impressions and instruction reach most deeply into a person's consciousness and personality. Here the influence of the mother is often paramount, and so special provision was made for the selection of a suitable mate. Clearly the men had proved unfaithful in setting aside the wives who could have reared another generation of priests (Mal 2:11, 15) and in failing to teach their children even the language in which worship must be conducted. In short, they had forfeited all the things that gave them a distinctive identity and mission (Ezek 44:10-16).

Ezra called them to rethink marriages that had deprived their lives of meaning and purpose, denied them a sense of spiritual worth and rectitude. The marriages had drawn religious leaders away from the covenant community and concomitantly produced children who had no knowledge of God's ways or of Israel's distinctive role among the nations. Levites and priests alike had forgotten their sacred trust to preserve the worship of the true and living God. Theirs was a hereditary office, passed from parents to children, to render to God praise and service and to regulate the cult of Yahweh. In their dual role as priests and public health officers, they had a responsibility to the entire community (Num 1:53; 3:7; 8:19).

If the men were to maintain their membership in the covenant community, they must end the marriages that had caused them to rupture their ties with the people and purposes of God. Thus under the direction of Ezra, those who had broken faith committed themselves to a new covenant that required them to put away their heathen families and to give their sons and daughters in marriage only to those in the community of faith (Ezra 10:1-14). Careful provision was made for the women and their children who were being returned to their own society (10:12-17), and the husbands were restored to a place among God's people.

Considering the Community

The account suggests that divorce must also be considered in relationship to the wider community, the couple's children and others beyond the family. If a marriage endangers the physical, emotional, social or spiritual welfare of others, then there must be sober reflection on the consequences of continuing the union. If all of one's energy must be expended on maintaining a relationship that is a violation of God's purposes and provision, one must think through what it is that gives meaning to life.

Seldom do we mention the covenant that was based on divorce. It was far from an optimal arrangement, but this harsh step was the least undesirable solution to a terrible problem. One of the purposes of the covenant is the perpetuation of a "godly seed" (see Mal 2:15). In considering an action of divorce, the welfare of the children must be given a high priority. The purposes of the biblical covenants again and again involve the entire people and their progeny. Consigning children to lives of terror and abuse is a violation of the biblical intent for marriage and the home.

We need to look carefully at what Jesus says about divorce. He was confronted by legalistic Pharisees who wished to embroil him in an ongoing argument (Mt 19:3-9; Mk 10:2-12). The issue was a source of lively debate among the rabbinic scholars of the day. The school of Shammai maintained that only for adultery could a woman be divorced, while the school of Hillel had derived a whole battery of reasons justifying putting away one's wife—including finding another woman who was more attractive. Other bases for divorce included burning a man's dinner, spinning in the street, having untidy hair, even a dog bite that did not heal. A major objective was to find a pretext for a man to send away his wife but retain her dowry.

In this context Jesus vehemently condemned the practice. His saying in the Sermon on the Mount likewise contains responses to the religious establishment's decrees "You have heard it said . . . but I say to you" (Mt 5:21, 27, 31, 33, 38, 43). The system itself created patterns of adultery, divorce and remarriage that wreaked havoc in souls. Divorce was carried out at the man's discretion, and there were few options for a woman but to be given to another, in either marriage or prostitution. This was not God's purpose in the creation of male and female given to one another to reflect the glory of God in lives of loving commitment.

Christ's purpose was not to create a legalism that would lock people into life-threatening situations. Indeed it was his repudiation of legalism that caused the Pharisees to hate him. He maintained that the sabbath was made for people rather than people for the sabbath, that it was legitimate for the near-starving David to eat the holy showbread. We need to look beyond legalism to the purposes of God's life-bringing law. As Jesus quoted Isaiah 29:13—"In vain do they worship me, teaching human precepts as doctrines"—he added "You abandon the commandment of God and hold to human tradition" (Mk 7:7-8). Can meaningful marriages be built on violence, bloodshed and wickedness?

The New Testament gives two exceptions in which divorce is approved. The first is given by Jesus: the case of *porneia* (Mt 5:32; 19:9). This word can mean any sort of inappropriate sexual attitude or action, whether fornication, adultery, prostitution or sexual abuse. A second exception is given by Paul in 1 Corinthians 7:10-16.

Paul addresses those who have come to Christ and find themselves married to an unbeliever. He declares that those who do divorce should not remarry another (v. 11)—a clear indication that some divorces are taking place. The apostle instructs the Christian not to leave the marriage but not to compel the non-Christian to remain (vv. 12-16). The consideration is in part the matter of relationship to the whole community of faith. If union with a believer causes a prostitute to have a relationship with the body of Christ (1 Cor 6:15), how much more a legitimately married spouse? We are told the partner is sanctified and the children holy (1 Cor 7:14). Here it is assumed that the children are being raised with an understanding of the gospel and its claims on their lives. Adherence to the community standards may well have aggravated an unsympathetic spouse: patterns of worship, acts of charity, hospitality to strangers and gifts to the poor. Paul's implication is not that the spouse should desist from the requirements of Christian discipleship but that their fulfillment might be repugnant to a nonbeliever.

Called to Peace

The Ezra-Nehemiah episode requires divorce in order to preserve the integrity of the covenant community. First Corinthians 7 attempts to bring a peaceful resolution to a troubled conflict involving matters of faith and practice. This passage is well worth considering, especially in situations where all the covenantal aspects of marriage have been lost, whether through infidelity, desertion or abuse. A marriage of abuse cannot be a marriage reflecting Christ's love for the church. Paul comments that "in such a case a brother or sister is not bound" (1 Cor 7:15). *Douleuō*, the word translated as "bound," literally means to serve in bondage as a slave. We might translate "a sister or brother is not held captive in such circumstances, for God has called you to peace." The need for peace must be prayerfully considered.

All of us earnestly desire that troubled marriages be healed, but the option of divorce should be recognized. Often indeed the contemplation of divorce has a very curative effect on one or both partners in a painful marriage. To declare that divorce is not an option is to deprive believers of an avenue that the Bible holds open.[2]

13

Our Global
Responsibility

Through the prophet Isaiah God promised, "My people will abide in a peaceful habitation, in secure dwellings, and in quiet resting places" (Is 32:18). But when will the promise be fulfilled? Do we just wait or do we work for that fulfillment? The director of Help for Abused Women and Children encourages us: "Unlike many social problems that afflict vulnerable people, domestic abuse can be prevented and ultimately ended. But it will take a ground-swell from people like yourselves."

If those in the wider community realize this potential, what can be expected from God's people? The Bible tells us that God has made us competent as ministers of a new covenant—not of the letter but of the Spirit; for the letter kills, but the Spirit gives life (2 Cor 3:6).

The implications cannot be avoided. If God has made us competent ministers, then we must declare God's love and empowerment of all persons. We must insist that our spiritual leaders point to ways of life rather than death. When violence against women ranks as the foremost public health problem in America, we must demand that the problem be addressed from the pulpit. When the United Nations declares that it is the most widespread form of violence throughout the globe, God's people must take notice.

Concerted Voice and Action

It is the duty of the true prophet to identify wrongdoing and to denounce it, though the false prophet condones bloodshed and violence. Furthermore, the Bible teaches that abuse within the church family is most certainly our business and that we must adopt a very hard line against it.

There are many forms of violence against women, some practiced in specific areas of the world or in specific cultures. But all abusive practices are the concern of all of God's people. If one suffers, we all suffer (1 Cor 12:16). Our concerted voice around the world can effect what more localized protests may not.

A case in point is the abolition of foot-binding in China. This age-old practice of hampering the free movement of women was discarded far more rapidly than students of culture might have expected. Families, and women in particular, covenanted together not to take wives with bound feet for their sons, nor to give in marriage daughters with bound feet. When entire groups held each other accountable to honor the agreement, the custom was abandoned at a remarkable speed.

Covenanting among families and faith groups might also bring an end to genital mutilation. At present men in certain parts of Africa are reluctant to take brides who have not been circumcised, and a woman's family fears that failure to circumcise her will prevent her from finding a willing husband. If we are to overcome the horror of genital mutilation, Christians must raise a concerted voice. They must speak out against the pain, infection, hemorrhaging and misery occasioned by female circumcision, as well against the deprivation of women's physical joy of married love. The clitoris is unique among the organs of the body in being designed solely for pleasure. This joy-giving endowment of God must not be willfully destroyed, for mutilation is specifically forbidden in the Scriptures (Lev 19:28; 20:19; 21:5). Christians in every culture must bear witness and seek a unified stand a unified stand against such evil.

In India the church has condemned the practice of giving a dowry in order to counter a widespread abuse. An appalling number of women are killed each year as demands for increased dowry payment escalate. The family of the bride must meet the demand or risk the death of their daughter. Often a mother-in-law or sister-in-law contrives an accident that claims the life of a hapless bride. Termination of the dowry system is the best hope for abolition of this evil; activists are seeking to put in place an inheritance system for women that will obviate the need of a dowry. In the meantime many Christians—including pastors—flout the dowry prohibition and thereby perpetuate the custom. Direct denunciation can hardly be expected from a pastor who has been party to the system in his own family. The faithful witness of Christians coupled with worldwide censure can provide a prophetic voice that cannot be ignored.

The number of dowry deaths reported nation-wide in India rose from 5,513 in 1996 to 6,917 in 1998, the last year for which government records are available. Women's activists say the cases reflect only a fraction of the total such deaths, most of which, they say, are wrongly recorded as accidents.[1]

Proclaiming Women as Joint Heirs of God's Grace

There are other abuses that call for the prophetic voice of the church. Among these are sex trafficking, forced prostitution, forced abortion and child pornography. Many of these are predicated on the position that women are of little worth. A key factor in the spread of AIDS in Africa is said to be the low valuation of women. We must be very clear that God has bestowed on women equal dignity and honor. This proclamation is necessary to a world where women can be slain simply to vindicate the honor of their male relatives.

"A woman in Arab societies is an object for sex and reproduction. As long as she is an object, she is owned by a father, a husband, a brother," says Salwa Bakr, an Egyptian feminist and writer. "The way she uses her body is not her business but the business of those who own her."[2]

The bodies of both women and men belong to the Savior who has redeemed them. Women are full spiritual beings in their own right, responsible to God for their actions and intentions. Throughout the earth we must bear witness that all persons are equal in Jesus Christ and all are worthy of respect and justice.

Keeping Each Other Honest

Western churches have a responsibility not to allow their teachings to be misconstrued or distorted in other parts of the world. Most tragic has been the exporting of American subordinationist doctrine, often in an especially harsh form, to churches in other parts of the world. Sociologist Eva Lundgren interviewed a group of Norwegian batterers, all of whom but one had been strongly influenced by American teaching on family roles. Lundgren asked them, "Does beating give you any positive openings? What possible positive reward do you get from beating?"

The replies were chilling. One responded: "I do hit her, of course I do, of course. Well, I've got to set limits. I've taken courses in Christian pedagogy; they've been extremely useful, because at those courses you learn about setting limits . . . so they learn where the limit goes."

And: "There are simply things that cannot be expressed in words, things that have to be supplemented with blows. . . . Hitting is the only language [my wife] understands, and that is important to say."[3]

We dare not countenance the export of teaching that endangers the lives and well-being of women and children. Neither can we countenance such teaching within our own church walls. A pastor friend told of hearing a visiting evangelist declare to the abused women in his audience, "Go back and take another beating!" Voices of protest must be raised. Controlling alarming teachings like this is everyone's responsibility. As the apostle taught us long ago, wrong doctrine that spreads "like gangrene" must be countered with faithful instruction in the Word (2 Tim 2:15-17; 3:16). Let us correct the error for the very honor of God's name!

A Shared Call

All over the world Christian families are under attack. The assault is launched with insults, injuries, demeaning humiliation, cursing, shouting, verbal and emotional abuse, blows, bloodshed and sexual violence. These come not from unbelievers outside the household of faith but from those inside the Christian fold. The oppressors are those who are nearest and dearest to the victims. This book aims to articulate a call for us to recognize the extent of abuse in Christian families and understand that we can and must address the problem. The Bible consistently pronounces God's judgment on those who use their power to inflict suffering on others. Conversely, great blessing is promised to those who use their power to alleviate the oppression and suffering of others. How will we respond to the challenge?

Appendix 1

God Speaks
Out Against Abuse

Scripture Passages & Principles

Developed by the World Evangelical Fellowship, Task Force on Abuse Against Women

☐ The Bible calls for loving, responsible relationships between members of the family, with each in honor and industry providing for the needs of the other (Ps 128:1-4; 133:1-3; 1 Tim 5:8).

☐ A wife is an equal heir of the grace of life and not the possession of her husband (1 Pet 3:7; 1 Cor 6:19-20).

☐ Intimacy requires equality and mutuality. Sexual communion requires mutual consent (Jn 10:33-35; 15:15; Mt 18:4; 23:11-12; Mk 9:35; 10:42-45; Lk 9:48; 1 Cor 7:3-4).

☐ God's plan is that the home should be free of oppression (Is 54:5-14; Rom 12:8).

☐ Physical violence and verbal abuse are forbidden by God (Ps 56:5-6; Is 58:4-6; Mt 5:22; 1 Thess 4:3-6).

☐ Misunderstanding of the concepts of headship, submission and hierarchy should not be used to justify abuse (Mt 20:25-28; Mk 10:42-45; 2 Pet 3:16).

☐ Silence, secrecy and concealment are not God's way of dealing with problems (Mt 10:26; Mk 4:22; Lk 8:17; 12:2-3; Eph 5:13-14; Jas 5:16).

☐ The church is charged with the responsibility to address situations of abuse within its own community (Mt 18:15-17; Gal 6:1; 1 Thess 5:14; 2 Thess 3:14-15; 1 Tim 4:20; Tit 3:10-11; Jas 5:19-20).

☐ Polygamy, adultery and infidelity are condemned in Scripture (Lev 18:20; 1 Cor 6:8; Heb 13:4).

☐ Christians cannot condone polygamy, prostitution, sex trafficking, child abuse or rape (1 Cor 6:9-10, 15-16; Eph 5:3-5; 1 Tim 3:2; Mt 18:1-6; Mk 9:42; Lk 17:1-2).

☐ Forgiveness is the work of the Holy Spirit. For the abuser, it must be preceded by true repentance. For the abused, forgiveness is part of the healing process and will take time and perhaps distance (1 Cor 7:10-11; Gal 5:22-23; 6:2; Jas 1:4; Gen 42:21-23; 45:4-15; 50:20; Rom 2:4).

☐ Changed attitude and behavior rather than tears, extravagant gifts or desperate promises bespeak genuine repentance (Mt 3:8; Lk 3:8; Acts 26:20; Heb 12:17).

☐ While Christians may in some circumstances risk their lives for the sake of the gospel, they should not be exhorted to remain or return to life-threatening situations that might be avoided (Rom 16:3-4; Mt 4:5-7; Acts 9:23-24; 12:17; 14:19-20; 17:5-10; 19:29-31; 23:10, 12-24).

☐ Sometimes separation is the best course for the safety and peace of family members (Gen 13:7-11; 14:8-16; 21:9-21; 25:8-9; 27:41-45; 32:1-33; 45:4-15; Prov 24:1-2; Acts 16:36-40; Col 4:10; Philem 24; 1 Cor 7:5).

☐ Godly men and women are called to acknowledge the prevalence and severity of abuse, to respond compassionately to those who suffer and to aid in their healing through practical and spiritual support (Is 58:6-7; Rom 12:15; Eccles 4:1).

☐ The church should be an agent of healing for the offender (Lk 4:16-21; Tit 2:15; Heb 12:12-13).

Team Members

Winnie Bartel, U.S.A. (chair)
Mary Bassali, Egypt
Esme Bower, South Africa
Janice Crouse, U.S.A.
Margaret Jacobs, Australia
Catherine Clark Kroeger, U.S.A.
Lee Eng Lee, Malaysia
Ksenja Magda, Croatia
Leela Manasseh, India

Judy Mbugua, Kenya
Gwen McVicker, Canada
Olly Mesach, Indonesia
Nancy Nason-Clark, Canada
Grace Nedelchev, Bulgaria
Sharon Payt, U.S.A.
Holly Sheldon, Singapore
Lucett Thomas, Costa Rica
Blossom White, Jamaica

Appendix 2

Scriptures That Condemn
Abuse & Offer
Comfort to Victims

Do not envy the violent
   and do not choose any of their ways. (Prov 3:31)

Do not envy the wicked,
   nor desire to be with them;
for their minds devise violence,
   and their lips talk of mischief. . . .
Whoever plans to do evil
   will be called a mischief-maker. . . .
If you faint in the day of adversity,
   your strength being small;
if you hold back from rescuing those taken away to death,
   those who go staggering to the slaughter;
if you say "Look, we did not know this"—
   does not he who weighs the heart perceive it?
Does not he who keeps watch over your soul know it?
   And will he not repay all according to their deeds? (Prov 24:1-2, 8, 10-12)

A bishop, as God's steward, must be blameless; he must not be arrogant or
quick-tempered or addicted to wine or violent or greedy for gain; but he must

be hospitable, a lover of goodness, prudent, upright, devout, and self-con-trolled. (Tit 1:7)

My friends, if anyone is detected in a transgression, you who have received the Spirit should restore such a one in a spirit of gentleness. Take care that you yourselves are not tempted. Bear one another's burdens, and in this way you will fulfill the law of Christ. (Gal 6:1-2)

Verbal Abuse and Its Consequences

You have heard that it was said to those of ancient times, "You shall not mur-der"; and "whoever murders shall be liable to judgment." But I say to you that if you are angry with a brother or sister, you will be liable to judgment; and if you insult a brother or sister, you will be liable to the council; and if you say, "You fool," you will be liable to the hell of fire. (Mt 5:21-23)

For all of us make many mistakes. Anyone who makes no mistakes in speak-ing is perfect, able to keep the whole body in check with a bridle. If we put bits into the mouths of horses to make them obey us, we guide their whole bodies. Or look at ships: though they are so large that it takes strong winds to drive them, yet they are guided by a very small rudder wherever the will of the pilot directs. So also the tongue is a small member, yet it boasts of great exploits.

How great a forest is set ablaze by a small fire! And the tongue is a fire. The tongue is placed among our members as a world of iniquity; it stains the whole body, sets on fire the cycle of nature, and is itself set on fire by hell. For every species of beast and bird, of reptile and sea creature, can be tamed and has been tamed by the human species, but no one can tame the tongue—a restless evil, full of deadly poison. With it we bless the Lord and Father, and with it we curse those who are made in the likeness of God. From the same mouth come blessing and cursing. My brothers and sisters, this ought not to be so. (Jas 3:2-10)

Of Sex and Saints

For this is the will of God, your sanctification: that you abstain from fornication; that each one of you know how to control your own body in holiness and honor, not with lustful passion, like the Gentiles who do not know God; that no one wrong or exploit a brother or sister in this matter, because the Lord is an avenger in all these things, just as we have already told you beforehand and solemnly warned you. For God did not call us to impurity but in holiness. (1 Thess 4:3-8)

Because of cases of sexual immorality, each man should have his own wife and each woman her own husband. The husband should give to his wife her conjugal rights, and likewise the wife to her husband. For the wife does not have authority over her own body, but the husband does; likewise the husband does not have authority over his own body, but the wife does. Do not deprive one another except perhaps by agreement for a set time, to devote yourselves to prayer, and then come together again, so that Satan may not tempt you because of your lack of self-control. (1 Cor 7:2-5)

If any of you put a stumbling block before one of these little ones who believe in me, it would be better for you if a great millstone were fastened around your neck and you were drowned in the depth of the sea. Woe to the world because of stumbling blocks! Occasions for stumbling are bound to come, but woe to the one by whom the stumbling block comes! (Mt 18:6-7)

When Tempted to Put Oneself or Another in a Life-Threatening Situation
Then the devil took him to Jerusalem, and placed him on the pinnacle of the temple, saying to him, "If you are the Son of God, throw yourself down from here, for it is written,
'He will command his angels concerning you,
to protect you,'
and
'On their hands they will bear you up,
so that you will not dash your foot against a stone.'"
Jesus answered him, "It is said, 'Do not put the Lord your God to the test.' "
(Lk 4:9-13)

God's Empathy with Abused Women
Your lovers despise you;
they seek your life.
For I heard a cry as of a woman in labor,
anguish as of one bringing forth her first child —
the cry of the Daughter of Zion gasping for breath,
stretching out her hands,
"Woe is me! I am fainting before murderers." (Jer 4:30-31)

They have healed the wound of my people lightly,
saying, "Peace, peace,"
when there is no peace. . . .

We looked for peace, but no good came,
 for a time of healing, but behold, terror. .
Hark, the cry of the daughter of my people
 from the length and breadth of the land:
"Is the LORD not in Zion? Is her King not in her?" . .
For the wound of the daughter of my people is my heart wounded.
 I mourn, and dismay has taken hold on me.
Is there no balm in Gilead?
 Is there no physician there?
Why then has the health of the daughter of my people
 not been restored?
O that my head were waters,
 and my eyes a fountain of tears,
that I might weep day and night
 for the slain of my people! (Jer 8:11, 15, 19, 21—9:1 RSV)

Reassurance for Abused Women
Out of my distress I called on the LORD;
 the LORD answered and set me in a broad place.
With the LORD on my side I do not fear.
 What can mortals do to me?
The LORD is on my side to help me;
 I shall look in triumph on those who hate me. (Ps 118:5-6)

The Prayer of One in Danger
Rescue me, O LORD, from evil men;
 protect me from men of violence,
who devise evil plans in their hearts
 and stir up war every day.
They make their tongues as sharp as a serpent's;
 the poison of vipers is on their lips.

Keep me, O LORD, from the hands of the wicked;
 protect me from men of violence
 who plan to trip my feet.
Proud men have hidden a snare for me;
 they have spread out the cords of their net
 and have set traps for me along my path.

O LORD, I say to you, "You are my God."
Hear, O LORD, my cry for mercy. (Ps 140:1-6 NIV)

Rescue me from my enemies, O LORD,
  for I hide myself in you.
Teach me to do your will,
  for you are my God;
may your good Spirit
  lead me on level ground.

For your name's sake, O LORD, preserve my life;
  in your righteousness, bring me out of trouble. (Ps 143:9-11 NIV)

A Victim's Feeling of Betrayal
My friends and companions avoid me because of my wounds;
  my neighbors stay far away. (Ps 38:11 NIV)

It is not enemies who taunt me—
  I could bear that;
it is not adversaries who deal insolently with me—
  I could hide from them.
But it is you, my equal,
  my companion, my familiar friend,
with whom I kept pleasant company;
  we walked in the house of God with the throng. ,
My companion laid hands on a friend
  and violated a covenant with me
with speech smoother than butter,
  but with a heart set on war;
with words that were softer than oil,
  but in fact were drawn swords. (Ps 55:12-14, 20-21)

The Pattern of True Godliness
Look, you serve your own interest on your fast day,
  and oppress all your workers.
Look, you fast only to quarrel and to fight
  and to strike with a wicked fist.
Such fasting as you do today
  will not make your voice heard on high.
Is such the fast that I choose,
  a day to humble oneself?
Is it to down the head like a bulrush,

and to lie in sackcloth and ashes?
Will you call this a fast,
      a day acceptable to the LORD?

Is not this the fast that I choose:
      to loose the bonds of injustice,
      to undo the thongs of the yoke,
to let the oppressed go free,
      and to break every yoke?
Is it not to share your bread with the hungry,
      and bring the homeless poor into your house;
when you see the naked, to cover them,
      and not to hide yourself from your own kin?
Then your light shall break forth like the dawn,
      and your healing shall spring up quickly;
your vindicator shall go before you,
      the glory of the LORD shall be your rear guard.
Then you shall call, and the LORD will answer;
      you shall cry for help, and he will say, Here I am.

If you remove the yoke from among you,
      the pointing of the finger, the speaking of evil,
if you offer food to the hungry
      and satisfy the needs of the afflicted,
then your light shall rise in the darkness
      and your gloom be like the noonday.
The LORD will guide you continually,
      and satisfy your needs in parched places,
      and make your bones strong;
and you shall be like a watered garden,
      like a spring of water,
      whose waters never fail. (Is 58:3-11)

The Call for God's People to Deliver the Oppressed from Violence
Thus says the LORD:
Execute justice in the morning,
      and deliver from the hand of the oppressor
      anyone who has been robbed,
or else my wrath will go forth like fire,

and burn, with no one to quench it,
because of your evil doings. . . .

Act with justice and righteousness, and deliver from the hand of the oppressor
anyone who has been robbed. And do no wrong or violence to the alien, the
fatherless, and the widow, or shed innocent blood in this place. . . .

Did not your father eat and drink
    and do justice and righteousness?
    Then it was well with him.
He judged the cause of the poor and the needy;
    then it was well.
Is not this to know me?
    says the LORD. (Jer 21:12, 22:3, 15-16)

Guidance for Husbands

Husbands, love your wives, just as Christ loved the church and gave himself
up for her, in order to make her holy by cleansing her with the washing of
water by the word, so as to present the church to himself in splendor, without
a spot or wrinkle or anything of the kind—yes, so that she may be holy and
without blemish. In the same way, husbands should love their wives as they
do their own bodies. He who loves his wife loves himself. For no one ever
hates his own body, but he nourishes and tenderly cares for it, just as Christ
does for the church, because we are members of his body. "For this reason a
man will leave his father and mother and be joined to his wife, and the two
will become one flesh." This is a great mystery, and I am applying it to Christ
and the church. Each of you, however, should love his wife as himself, and a
wife should respect her husband. (Eph 5:25-33)

Husbands, in the same way, show consideration for your wives in your life
together, paying honor to the woman as the weaker sex, since they too are
also heirs of the gracious gift of life—so that nothing may hinder your
prayers. (1 Pet 3:7)

Husbands, love your wives and never treat them harshly. (Col 3:19)

A Pattern for Wives

A capable wife who can find?
    She is far more precious than jewels.

The heart of her husband trusts in her,
  and he will have no lack of gain.
She does him good, and not harm,
  all the days of her life. . . .
Her husband is known in the city gates,
  taking his seat among the elders of the land. . .
She opens her mouth with wisdom,
  and the teaching of kindness is on her tongue.
She looks well to the ways of her household,
  and does not eat the bread of idleness. . . .
  A woman who fears the LORD is to be praised.
Give her a share in the fruit of her hands,
  and let her works praise her in the city gates.
        (Prov 31:10-12, 23, 26-27, 30-31)

True Repentance Necessitates Honest Reparation

[Jesus said,] "Zacchaeus, hurry and come down; for I must stay at your house today." So he hurried down and was happy to welcome him. All who saw it began to grumble and said, "He has gone to be the guest of one who is a sinner." Zacchaeus stood there and said to the Lord, "Look, half of my possessions, Lord, I will give to the poor; and if I have defrauded anyone of anything, I will pay back four times as much." Then Jesus said to him, "Today salvation has come to this house, because he too is a son of Abraham. For the Son of Man came to seek and to save the lost." (Lk 19:5-10)

Thieves must give up stealing; rather let them labor and work honestly with their own hands, so as to have something to share with the needy. (Eph 4:28)

Bring forth fruits worthy of repentance. (Mt 3:8)

A Pattern for Reconciliation

Do not fear, for you will not be ashamed;
  do not be discouraged, for you will not suffer disgrace;
for you will forget the shame of your youth,
  and the disgrace of your widowhood you will remember no more.
For your Maker is your husband,
  the LORD of hosts is his name;
the Holy One of Israel is your Redeemer,
  the God of the whole earth he is called.

For the LORD has called you
    like a wife forsaken and grieved in spirit,
like the wife of a man's youth when she is cast off,
    says your God.
For a brief moment I abandoned you,
    but with great compassion I will gather you.
In overflowing wrath for a moment
    I hid my face from you,
but with everlasting love I will have compassion on you,
    says the LORD, your Redeemer.

This is like the days of Noah to me:
    Just as I swore that the waters of Noah
    would never go over the earth,
so I have sworn that I will not be angry with you
    and will not rebuke you.
For the mountains may depart
    and the hills be removed,
but my steadfast love shall not depart from you,
    and my covenant of peace shall not be removed,
    says the LORD, who has compassion on you.

O afflicted one, storm-tossed and not comforted,
    I am about to set your stones in antimony,
    and lay your foundations with sapphires.
I will make your pinnacles of rubies,
    your gates of jewels,
    and all your walls of precious stones.
All your children shall be taught by the LORD,
    and great shall be the prosperity of your children.
In righteousness you shall be established;
    you shall be far from oppression, for you shall not fear;
    and from terror, for it shall not come near you.
If anyone stirs up strife,
    it is not from me;
whoever stirs up strife with you
    shall fall because of you. . . .
No weapon that is fashioned against you shall prosper,
    and you shall confute every tongue that rises against you in judgment.

This is the heritage of the servants of the LORD
  and their vindication from me, says the LORD. (Is 54:4-17)

Therefore, I will now allure her,
  and bring her into the wilderness,
  and speak tenderly to her.
From there I will give her her vineyards,
  and make the Valley of Achor a door of hope.
There she shall respond as in the days of her youth,
  as at the time when she came out of the land of Egypt.
  On that day, says the LORD, you will call me, "My husband," and no longer will you call me, "My Baal." For I will remove the names of the Baals from her mouth, and they shall be mentioned by name no more. I will make for you a covenant on that day with the wild animals, the birds of the air, and the creeping things of the ground; and I will abolish the bow, the sword, and war from the land; and I will make you lie down in safety. And I will take you for my wife forever; I will take you for my wife in righteousness and in justice, in steadfast love, and in mercy. I will take you for my wife in faithfulness; and you shall know the LORD. (Hos 2:14-20)

Appendix 3

Intervention
Resources for Pastors

Critical Questions to Ask a Woman in Crisis
These questions are designed for a pastor who has just been told about an
incident of abuse by a woman who is seeking his counsel.

Frequency and Severity of the Abuse
☐ Is this the first time an abusive episode has occurred? *See if she is willing to
talk about other instances of abuse in their relationship. Try to assess the frequency of
such acts and whether they have become more frequent over time.*
☐ Could you describe for me the behaviors that are part of the abuse? *Try to
assess the severity of the abuse and whether it is becoming more severe over time. It is
important to remember that verbal abuse can be very painful and has long-term consequences, just like physical forms of abuse.*

Safety
☐ Is it safe for you to return home at this time? Are your children safe in the
home?
☐ Do you have a safety plan? By that I mean some means by which to leave
your home quickly should it become unsafe for you or the children. Do you
have access to a car at all times? Is there public transportation close to where
you live, or taxi service?
☐ Do you know how to contact the transition house in our community if you

should decide to seek refuge there? *Make sure you have the name and telephone number of the transition house available as well as a brochure describing their services to give her if she would like it.*

☐ Has there ever been a time that your husband's anger frightened you or made you feel unsafe? Do you fear that your husband could harm himself or damage your property?

☐ If you have reason to become concerned about your own safety or the safety of your children, what can this church do to help you find a refuge? *Make sure that she leaves your office with a telephone number for use in case of emergency. If possible, have a small team of people who would be able and willing to assist in such an emergency so you do not have to shoulder this responsibility alone.*

Therapeutic Options

☐ Have you ever sought the help of a mental health professional, like a psychologist or psychiatrist? Are you aware of the differences in approach between a clinical psychologist, a psychiatrist and a social worker? *It is important for pastoral counselors to know what forms of assistance have been sought in the past and whether or not therapeutic intervention has been helpful.*

☐ Are you aware of the therapeutic resources available in our community? *It is important for clergy to know something about who is available, what their training or orientation to therapy is, how much experience they have in providing service to abuse victims, what they charge for services, their wait list, and whether they offer emergency services or twenty-four-hour crisis intervention.*

☐ Have you considered whether it might be a good idea to seek the help of a trained mental health professional in dealing with the pain of abuse? *Many religious people are reluctant to seek help outside of the faith community. Pastors can be an important bridge, linking the resources of the church and the resources of the community. A suggestion from a pastor can be powerful encouragement to seek help from a professionally trained counselor.*

Practical Support

☐ Are there day-to-day tasks that are difficult for you to complete at the moment?

☐ Do you have access to a car or transportation?

☐ Is there someone you could leave the children with if you needed to be free of childcare responsibilities for a few hours?

☐ Do you have sufficient food, and are your other material needs met?

☐ Are there ways that the church family could make daily living a bit easier? How?

The Children

☐ How is the crisis at home affecting your children? Are they aware of the frequency and severity of the abuse? *Children are seriously affected by witnessing abuse; watching their father batter their mother has a long-term impact on boys as well as girls.*

☐ Have you noticed any change in their school performance? *Sometimes it is helpful for a mother to talk to a teacher or other school personnel to see whether their child's school performance or social behavior has altered.*

☐ What do your children most need right now? *Many abused women do not fully understand how traumatic violent conflict between adults is for their children.*
Are there ways the church family could reach out to your children at this time? *It may be that the children would like to be involved in age-appropriate groups in the church but do not have a way to get there; a Sunday-school teacher or youth worker could be informed that the family is undergoing difficulties and alerted to be especially attentive to the child's needs. If you want to speak to church workers about the situation, you will need the mother's explicit permission to do so.*

Spiritual Issues

☐ How has the abuse you have suffered affected your relationship with God? with the church?

☐ Have you found some helpful Bible passages to read during this painful time? *You may want to offer the abused woman a brochure listing Scripture passages that focus on healing.*

☐ Have you been able to talk to God about the abuse you are suffering? *It may be appropriate to pray aloud for the abused woman, her healing journey, her children and hope for the future. Your prayer can be a model of how she herself could talk to God about her life and her suffering.*

☐ Do you feel supported by your church family during this period of crisis? *Explore her expectations of the church, the pastor and the people, and assess whether she has been disappointed or uplifted by responses to her suffering. If she has been disappointed, try to determine how the church might fill in the gaps in the days and months to come.*

Dealing with a Man Who Is Abusive

As a pastor, you need to realize that anything that you say to an abusive man can have a direct impact on the woman he is abusing. Listed below are some issues of which you need to be particularly mindful. These are questions to ask yourself.

Misinterpretation of Your Words

Is there anything I am saying that could be misinterpreted as support for abuse or as downplaying the seriousness of the violence? *It is common for abusers to downplay the harm they have caused to the victim and their children. They will often attempt to manipulate a pastor to minimize the significance of their actions or exaggerate the sincerity of their promises to change.*

If the woman has sought temporary refuge in a shelter or another safe environment, is there anything I am saying that could be misinterpreted as support for her to return home prematurely? *Abusers usually do not want to separate from the victim and will go to great lengths to ensure that she does not leave the home or that she returns home quickly. Promises to change and changed behavior are not the same thing.*

Is there anything I am saying that could be used to justify the latest act of violence or to suggest that the victim herself is at fault for the abuse she has suffered? *Abusers will often deny or downplay the seriousness of their offenses. Sometimes they suggest that the victim provoked the violence and is thus responsible for it.*

Potential Danger

Have I met alone with the victim of violence to ensure that I have heard fully the history and circumstances surrounding the abuse? *Most often it is not advisable for a pastor to meet with an abuser and a victim together. Even if they come for counsel together, the wise pastor will ensure that the victim's story is told independently of the abuser's story. Meeting with them together can threaten the victim's safety.*

Do I realize that anything I say to the perpetrator might be used at some point against the victim? *It is not uncommon for an abuser to use the words of a pastor to try to convince his victim to come back home or to accept his plea for forgiveness independent of changed behavior.*

Have I considered fully the potential risk of danger to the victim and her children? *Never forget that the man who has caused harm and injuries to the victim may well be pleasant, friendly and helpful in the church.*

Have I taken appropriate steps to ensure that I do not put myself as a pastoral counselor at undue risk or compromise the safety of my family? *Many police officers are threatened or injured after intervening in domestic violence. Pastors need to be aware of the danger involved in responding to a crisis call when abuse is occurring. Normally it is not advisable to go unescorted into a volatile situation.*

If the victim has sought refuge in a shelter or another safe environment, do I understand fully that disclosing her whereabouts would put a number of people at enormous risk? *Clergy must not disclose to an abuser the location or contact number of the shelter where a victim and her family have sought refuge.*

Do I realize that the abuser may try to manipulate me to reunite the family or to convince the victim to return home prematurely? *There is often a hidden agenda when an abuser seeks help from a pastor shortly after an abusive incident has occurred, or when his victim has left the home for refuge elsewhere.*

Am I too ready to assume that a batterer who says he is sorry is truly repentant? *Tears and extravagant gifts are no substitutes for changed behavior. Abused women want the violence to stop not temporarily but forever.*

Have I considered the abuser's deep internal wounds? *Many men who batter their wives were childhood victims of abuse. As a result, they may have some deep psychological problems for which they need professional help. This does not excuse the abuse but is the context from which it needs to be understood. Abusers need help from the pastor and from community programs. They need to stop the violence and to get assistance in beginning life anew, free from the violent and controlling behavior that characterized their past.*

Making Sure Victims Get the Help They Need
How You Might Encourage the Victim of Abuse
I am deeply honored that you have shared your life story with me. I am saddened by the suffering you have endured, but I commend you for the courage to speak about what has happened in your home. The time has come to look for healing and recovery. As a church, we want to walk with you as you search for wholeness and a new start. Our God is the God of hope and new oeginnings.

I also want to encourage you to take advantage of the resources we have available in our community to assist you on the road to healing and wholeness. As your pastor I hope we can work together so that the future will be much brighter than the past.

I do not know whether you are aware of the various agencies and professionals who might be of assistance to you. You have mentioned a number of legal questions to me and also some concerns you have about the children. These are beyond my area of expertise, but I would be happy to put you in contact with someone who would be better equipped than I to answer them. Would you like me to suggest a couple of people you could contact directly, or would you like me to make an inquiry on your behalf?

Sample Contact with a Psychologist
My name is Jared Smith, and I am the pastor of Cedar Glen Community Church in Washville. A woman in my congregation has recently disclosed to me that she has been the victim of wife abuse. I have discussed with her a number of therapeutic options available in our community, and she has

decided that she would like an appointment to see a clinical psychologist. I am calling to inquire about your availability and how she might be able to access your services.

Sample Contact with a Transition House
I am calling to ask whether a member of the staff of Greenhill House might be available to meet with the crisis intervention team of our church, First Baptist of Bridge Street. As the new senior pastor, I am wanting to get connected with the resources available in our community so that in the event that an abused woman comes to us for help, I will have information about the shelter and names of some workers there whom she might contact. In my previous parish we had brochures from the local transition house posted inside the women's washrooms and available on our display table. We would be so grateful for the opportunity to meet with workers at your house and to hear about how our congregation could be involved in helping to stop violence in our community.

Assessing What Resources Are Available in Your Community
Batterers' Support Group
When a case of abuse is prosecuted, sometimes the courts will mandate therapy for the abuser, or attendance at a batterers' support group or anger-management group. Sometimes health care professionals encourage men to attend such a group. Groups usually run for a designated period of time under the leadership of a social worker or trained counselor.

Legal Help
Legal advice can help a woman answer questions such as the following: Is there any legal way to get my abusive husband to leave our home temporarily? How useful is a restraining order for ensuring my safety? If I leave our home for a few days or a few weeks, can he stop me from returning? What is a legal separation? What are the issues of child custody I might need to consider? What are the steps in seeking a divorce?

Medical Assistance
A physician can document the extent and severity of physical abuse and offer a woman help in exploring the physical components of her healing journey. The physician can answer questions like the following: What are the nature and extent of my injuries? Will full recovery be possible? How long should I expect the physical healing to take? How has living in an abusive home exac-

erbated my other physical problems? Are there physical signs or symptoms I should watch for as I struggle with ongoing difficulties?

Police
When physical safety is in jeopardy, the police are often the most equipped to help. Many police departments have a team specially trained to respond to domestic crises. Police officers can address concerns such as these: How will the police intervene if I call for their help? What are the steps in having a violent husband temporarily removed from the home? If charges are brought, how does the process develop from that point onward? What is the role of a restraining order, and do restraining orders work?

Psychologist/Psychiatrist
A clinical psychologist or psychiatrist can address the victim's need for restored mental and emotional health. Abuse extracts an enormous psychological cost. In the aftermath of living with an abusive partner, women usually find they need help with layers of emotional pain. A psychologist or psychiatrist can shed light on questions like these: What are some of the warning signs of poor mental health that I should be aware of in myself and in my children? How can I begin to gain control over my life and my choices? When will the despair and hopelessness I feel begin to lift? What combination of prescribed medications and therapy would best address my current problems? How can I protect myself in the future?

School-Based Services
A variety of services may be available through schools or the school district offices. Given the stresses and difficulties children experience living in, or separating from, an abusive environment, they often have difficulties at school and a decline in academic performance. The school's guidance counselor, social worker or psychologist can help children deal with their social and academic difficulties. The child's home-room teacher may need to be alerted to the home troubles; she or he can provide a referral to the school-based services. Individual counseling may be offered, and the counselor may work with the child's teachers to help provide a less stressful learning environment.

Social Assistance
A social worker can explore the steps necessary to access temporary benefits from the state, such as welfare or emergency relief. Social workers can help the abuse victim determine the following: Am I eligible for financial help if I

leave my husband and our home on a temporary or permanent basis? What is the waiting period for benefits? Is there a program to help me seek employment opportunities? Is there a retraining program for women who have been full-time homemakers for many years? If I work part time, do I still qualify for assistance to help pay for rent and food? What are the community options for low-income housing? What are the child-custody implications of leaving an abusive environment? Could applying for social assistance benefits trigger a home visitation for suspected child abuse?

Transition House/Shelter

Workers at a transition house are trained to meet the needs of an abused woman in crisis. While the standard length of stay differs from one shelter to another, the maximum stay is usually three to six months. Some communities also have second-stage housing, where women and their children can go after they leave the shelter. Here the maximum length of stay is approximately eighteen months to two years. Counseling is available in most shelters, and often there are programs for the children. No payment is expected in a transition house, though often there is some expectation that residents will assist with meal preparation and cleaning. Shelter workers are usually very well informed about the variety of services available to meet the emotional, legal and housing needs of residents.

Self-Help Groups

Many communities have self-help groups or victim-support small groups, perhaps organized through a mental health clinic, community service agency, church or hospital. Victims come together on a regular basis (usually every two weeks or once a month) to discuss their needs, report on their progress, and seek advice and support from others who have experienced abuse. One of the benefits is that the victim becomes aware that she is not alone in her struggle to overcome the pain of the past and the despair of the present. Some groups obtain the services of a professionally trained adviser, while others are completely autonomous.

Appendix 4

Educational Resources

Checklist for Premarital Counseling Sessions
It is critical for pastors to discuss the issue of abuse with all couples wishing to be married. It needs to be approached sensitively and without embarrassment. The following questions should be asked in individual sessions, apart from the partner.

Presence of Abuse
Everyone has to deal with disappointment, frustration and anger from time to time. Sometimes individuals or couples have a lot of trouble knowing how to handle differences of opinion, conflict, deep disappointment, frustration, or feelings of anger. Has either of you ever used physical means like pushing, hitting or punching as a strategy to assert control or to get your own way? Has there been any dating violence in your relationship? How did you respond to this? Are these events an ongoing cause of concern to you? Do you have any reason to believe it will not happen again?

Potential of Abuse
Sometimes physical abuse begins as verbal putdowns or name calling. Other times it begins during a very stressful period of life, like unemployment, financial trouble or pregnancy. No matter whether you can identify factors making

life challenging or difficult, abuse must never be excused or tolerated. It is important to seek the help and support of trained people should abuse occur in your relationship. I want to be sure you understand that the church wants to be a safe place to disclose abuse. Our God does not condone violence. The church family and I want to help all of the individuals connected with our church and our community to live free of any threat of abuse. Violence extracts an enormous cost. It must not be allowed to flourish or exist among us. Do you have any questions or comments to make about this?

This is a good opportunity to give information about abuse or to inform the woman or the man where they can find help in the future.

Sample Sermon Outline: Christian Family Life Should Be Free of Abuse

1. Illustrative stories. John and Sarah have been married for twenty-eight years, and during most of that time they have been desperately unhappy. He calls her degrading names, and during the winter months when he is out of work he often gets very angry and sometimes resorts to hitting or pushing her to get his own way. As a result, Sarah has become depressed, feeling that she is worth little in or outside of her home. She comes to church on Sunday mornings alone, and during the week she sticks pretty close to the farm. There are very few times that Sarah is seen with anyone besides her husband.

The Butterworths are a middle-aged couple, both teachers, who are relatively new converts to evangelical Christianity. They have three small children, and their lives revolve around their work and the needs of their family. Mrs. Butterworth was sexually abused as a child, and she suffers from low self-esteem. Her first marriage was abusive, and now she is trying very hard to rebuild her life with a new husband and a new faith. But she gets easily discouraged and finds that her past still haunts her present.

2. Statistics. The statistics listed here apply to the United States; pastors in other regions of the world will obviously want to choose data that relates to their own country.

☐ In the United States, ten women are killed by batterers every day; almost three-quarters of these murders occur after the woman has left the relationship, sought a restraining order or begun divorce proceedings (Seager 1997).

☐ The U.S. surgeon general reports that domestic violence is the greatest single cause of injury among American women, accounting for more emergency room visits than traffic accidents, muggings and rape combined <www.weaveinc.org/facts.html>.

☐ There are nearly three times as many animal shelters in the United States as there are shelters for battered women and their dependent children.

☐ The first battered woman's shelter was opened in the United States in St. Paul, Minnesota, in 1974 (Senate Judicial Hearings 1990).

☐ In the United States, 30 percent of women murdered are killed by their husbands, ex-husbands or boyfriends (U.S. Department of Justice 1995).

☐ According to a study reported in the *New England Journal of Family Medicine*, a handgun in the home is forty-three times more likely to kill a family member or an acquaintance than an intruder (<www.ncadv.org/problem.htm>).

3. Scripture readings. The Word of the Lord to the victim of violence:
Deliver me, O LORD, from evildoers;
> protect me from those who are violent. (Ps 140:1)

My God, my rock, in whom I take refuge,
> my shield and the horn of my salvation,
> my stronghold and my refuge,
> my savior; you save me from violence. (2 Sam 22:3)

From oppression and violence he redeems their life;
> and precious is their blood in his sight. (Ps 72:14)

As for what others do, by the word of your lips
> I have avoided the ways of the violent.
My steps have held fast to your paths;
> my feet have not slipped.
I call upon you, for you will answer me, O God;
> incline your ear to me, hear my words. (Ps 17:4-6)

The Word of the Lord to the congregation:
Do not envy the violent
> and do not choose any of their ways. (Prov 3:31)

Now a bishop must be above reproach, married only once, temperate, sensible, respectable, hospitable, an apt teacher, not a drunkard, not violent but gentle, not quarrelsome, and not a lover of money. (1 Tim 3:2)

O let the evil of the wicked come to an end,
> but establish the righteous,
you who test the minds and hearts,
> O righteous God. (Ps 7:9)

Why do you make me see wrongdoing
    and look at trouble?
Destruction and violence are before me;
    strife and contention arise. (Hab 1:3)

The Word of the Lord to abusers:
Therefore pride is their necklace;
    violence covers them like a garment. (Ps 73:6)

They eat the bread of wickedness
    and drink the wine of violence. (Prov 4:17)

For their minds devise violence,
    and their lips talk of mischief. (Prov 24:2)

Put away violence and oppression, and do what is just and right. (Ezek 45:9)

I hate . . . covering one's garment with violence, says the LORD of hosts. So take heed to yourselves and do not be faithless. (Mal 2:16)

4. Prayer
Creator God:
We ask, O Lord,
that you would open our eyes to see
the suffering of women around the world.
Give us ears to hear their cries
and hearts that will not rest
until we have done our part
to apply the healing balm of Gilead
to their wounds.
Amen.

5. Points to consider. You may wish to focus on the following questions:
☐ Where do we find violence in our culture?
☐ How can we recognize it in family life?
☐ What is the impact of abuse in the life of a woman, a man or a child?
☐ When are we, the body of Christ, going to take abuse seriously?
Your listeners should also consider the following:
☐ Family crisis is often hidden behind the closed doors of the family home

and the sweet Sunday smile of its members.

☐ A listening ear of a Christian friend or pastor is often the first step to transforming a life full of pain and despair.

☐ The informal support of the people of faith, expressed in individual acts of kindness, goes a long way toward empowering men and women to begin life anew.

☐ The social and emotional needs of church members are far greater than pastors' ability to assist. Congregations need to learn how to respond to needs both inside and outside the walls of the church.

☐ The shrinking social safety net in the public sector has provided new opportunities for churches and community resources to work as partners in alleviating the temporal suffering of men and women. We can learn to work together in cooperative ways that do not compromise our message of hope.

6. The challenge. Transforming the world for Christ—the responsibility of every believer—usually begins on home territory. It happens at the kitchen table, on the racquetball court, at thirty thousand feet in an airline's economy section, in the church building, in the women's shelter, the makeshift hospital or the soup kitchen.

Each of us need to make a pledge to ourselves and to God that we will strive to think and act in a manner consistent with our high view of the family. Such a pledge could turn the world upside down. And as we enter the twenty-first century, our world, its values and its priorities could use a good shakedown!

7. Questions to ponder. You will of course want to adapt these questions to make them appropriate for the region of the world in which you minister.

☐ What are the greatest needs of victims of violence in our community?

☐ How can we become a caring congregation?

☐ What can we do to reduce violence in our midst and within our neighborhoods?

☐ As a Christian who wants to lead a godly life and be helpful to others, how can I begin to meet the needs of suffering men, women and children in our community?

Appendix 5

Bible Studies
for Groups

Sacred as Salt
Women Ministering to Each Other

Mary is an eighty-year-old woman who lives with her eldest daughter, Sue. Sue's husband, Raymond, is very resentful of the intrusion of his mother-in-law, resulting in their lost privacy and the financial and emotional responsibilities of caring for someone who is frail. Sometimes he treats Mary harshly, saying words that pierce her heart or withholding access to her money. At night Mary can hear Raymond shouting at Sue, and sometimes she thinks she can hear Sue crying. As a result, Mary can hardly wait to die.

Peggy is a very bright and attractive eighteen-year-old in her first year of training to be a nurse. Her boyfriend, Jim, who works as a car mechanic, is very impatient with Peggy's educational aspirations and wants her to marry him now. He claims that all his friends are sleeping with their girlfriends and Peggy should be willing to have sex with him. As a Christian, Peggy is uncomfortable with the idea of sleeping with Jim before they are married. Last week he forced himself on her, despite her pleas. Peggy is frightened and very confused.

Kim, a mother of two preschoolers, just turned twenty-three. She was repeatedly abused by her husband and on two occasions required emergency medical treatment. She is now living on her own, but her dreams and self-confidence have been shattered. Lonely and afraid, Kim begins to attend a church near her home. Everyone there seems so happy; she hopes some of their joy will rub off on her.

1. Read the story of Dorcas (Acts 9) or the stretcher bearers (Mk 2) as an introduction to helping others..

2. Scripture verse for meditation: "You are the salt of the earth; but if salt has lost its taste, how can its saltiness be restored? It is no longer good for anything, but is thrown out and trampled under foot" (Mt 5:13).

3. Reflect on what it means to be the salt of the earth.

☐ In many parts of the Western world, summer is a time of rest and relaxation, but it is also a time of preparation for the long months of winter. Our foremothers knew, only too well, that if the family wanted to enjoy jam or pickles when the snow was falling, the jars needed to be prepared and filled when the sun was shining. By our love and care, we can help to prepare and preserve the life of someone else.

☐ In coastal communities many men and women make their living by fishing the waters and "salting the catch." Applying salt to the raw fish prevents it from spoiling or decaying: it extends its shelf life and ultimately enables the feeding of hungry people far away from the village where the fishing vessel was unloaded. As Christian women we can act as salt, preserving and preventing spoil through compassion and Christlike conduct.

☐ Salt has a medicinal quality. It promotes healing. As women motivated to serve Christ and those around us, we can be involved in binding up the wounds of each other. Just as the good Samaritan cared for the man at the roadside, we need to see those in need as we walk along the road of life. *Whose wounds might I bind up, Lord?*

☐ As the winter winds blow and water freezes in the northern corners of the globe, handfuls of coarse salt are thrown on walkways to melt the ice. Salt acts as a deicer, making treacherous pathways safe. As mothers, many of us are committed to calming the rough waters in the lives of our children. Christ commanded us to look out for the difficulties that others experience. *How can I calm someone else's storm, Lord?*

☐ People add salt to their food to enhance its flavor. Why do potatoes taste so much better to children when they are served as French fries or potato chips? Because of the large quantity of salt that has been added. Our service to God involves building up the body of Christ, enhancing the self-esteem and self-worth of others, helping them to recognize their gifts and prompting them to use those gifts in the church and beyond. *Whom, O Lord, can I build up?*

☐ Healthy choices made early in a young person's life can protect them against many of the harmful effects of living in the contemporary world. As women of faith we can act as a preservative in the lives of others. What a wonderful opportunity this opens up for us. Through our compassion and love, we can help to insulate someone else from future pain or suffering. As a car seatbelt offers some protection on the highway, my life might be able to preserve someone from danger. *To whom might I offer protection, Lord?*

4. Consider the challenge.

As women of faith, we can make a difference in our world. The gospel message commands us to be salt and light to a dark and often unsavory world. By binding up wounds, making rough paths smooth, adding flavor and acting as a preservative, we can make our presence felt at work, in the schools of our children, and with our neighbors. When we kiss a scraped knee, take an abused woman for an outing, help a sister in the faith believe in herself, or write a note to a teenager away at college, we are displaying "saltiness." How can you and I get out of the saltshaker?

5. Brainstorm on how to be salty in regard to abuse.

Ask group members to think aloud about how they might put Matthew 5:13 into practice in response to abuse in our world. Have them call out ideas for individual action or to do together as a group.

6. Prayer and offering.

Allow time for group members to prayerfully consider what her offering should be. Then have each woman write on a slip of paper one action that she is prepared to offer and place it in the offering plate. Close the meeting with a prayer from Psalm 7:9 (NIV):

> O righteous God,
> who searches minds and hearts,
> bring to an end the violence of the wicked
> and make the righteous secure.

Does God Say Anything About Dating Violence? A Discussion for Teens
Susan and Jim have been dating for about two years. They are regular youth-group attenders, both from church families. Susan is a pretty young woman who is quite shy and unsure of her talent and her future. Jim is very confident; with a pretty girlfriend, he is sure the future looks bright indeed. When he encounters frustration or disappointment, however, he gets quite angry. Jim's anger frightens Susan. She has seen him punch another guy in the face, and she has heard him verbally abuse his mother. Last week he pushed her

against a wall when she refused to finish one of his school assignments for him. She used to assume his outbursts were normal expressions of frustration, but he has been erupting more often of late, and this scares her.

Brenda and Billy are rather new to the church and to the youth group. They show a great deal of physical affection in public, sometimes making other teens feel a bit uncomfortable. In private Billy always demands more and more sexual intimacy, and he threatens to break up with Brenda if she does not comply. Not long ago he forced himself on Brenda despite her pleas. Later he apologized for making her cry and hurting her body. She wishes she could just run away.

1. Offer some guidelines to help teens assess their own relationships. It is not a positive relationship when he

☐ belittles you, makes fun of you, your clothing or your makeup
☐ makes you feel uncomfortable
☐ slaps, pushes, kicks or hurts you
☐ is verbally abusive
☐ has temper tantrums
☐ ignores your "no"
☐ does not value your opinion
☐ expects sexual favors in return for paying for a date
☐ threatens you
☐ pressures you to do something you do not want to do
☐ disrespects you, your family or your friends
☐ swears at you
☐ isolates you from your family or friends
☐ is extremely possessive or jealous
☐ blames you for his problems
☐ declares his love for you within a short time of beginning to date
☐ insists on being with you all the time

2. Offer suggestions for personal change or to assist a friend. If he is abusive:

☐ break off the relationship
☐ take time to heal
☐ seek positive friendships
☐ avoid being alone with him
☐ look for help
☐ talk to your parent(s), sister or brother, youth leader, pastor, teacher, coach, counselor or doctor—these people can listen, give advice and be supportive of your decisions

If a friend is suffering from abuse in a dating relationship:
- [ ] listen
- [ ] do not blame
- [ ] do not ignore the signs of abuse
- [ ] be supportive
- [ ] give encouragement
- [ ] be a shoulder to lean on
- [ ] offer to go with her for help
- [ ] invite her to go places with you
- [ ] ask for help to deal with her problems

3. Bible passages for study or reflection.

- [ ] Mark 2:1-12: Friends bringing friends to Jesus.
- [ ] 1 Corinthians 13:4-7: What does love look like?
- [ ] Luke 12:24-28: Are we not more valuable than the sparrows and the lilies to God?

Appendix 6

Resources for a Congregation

Critical Questions for a Lay Leader or Friend to Ask a Woman in Crisis

Safety

☐ Are you frightened to return home?

☐ Do you feel in danger? In what way?

☐ Have you ever called the police or considered calling the police?

Temporary Refuge

☐ Do you have somewhere you can go with your children if you are too frightened to return home or if you need to flee in a hurry?

☐ Do you know about the local transition house and the services they offer?

☐ Do you have a way to get there if you need to?

Children

☐ Do you have any particular concerns about the safety or welfare of your children? What are they?

Support

☐ Do you have people you can turn to when you feel you need to share what is happening in your life?

□ If you had an appointment with your doctor, a counselor or a lawyer, is there someone you could ask to come with you?

Practical Help
□ Are there some day-to-day tasks that are difficult for you to get done right now?
□ Do you have access to a car or transportation?
□ Is there someone you could leave the children with if you needed to be free of childcare responsibilities for a few hours?

Spiritual Help
□ Have you thought about how the church, our pastor or other Christian people could be helpful at this difficult point in your life?
□ Are there any specific spiritual needs that you wish someone could assist you with at this time?

Professional Help
□ Do you know whom to contact if you need legal help or a doctor's care?
□ If you felt the need for help from a professional therapist, would you know how to get it?

Immediate Needs
□ Have you thought of developing a safety plan (important documents copied, extra cash, telephone numbers of agencies or contacts) in case you need to leave your home very quickly?
□ Can I help connect you to those in our church or our community who are trained to help women coping with life crises?

Responding to Abuse: Phone Numbers and Contacts
You may wish to photocopy these pages for the use of church staff and lay leaders.

Members of the Church Emergency Response Team
Name_____ Tel._____
Name_____ Tel._____
Name_____ Tel._____
Name_____ Tel._____

Legal Services
Name_____ Tel._____
Name_____ Tel._____

Medical Services
Name_____ Tel._____
Name_____ Tel._____

Police
Name_____ Tel._____
Name_____ Tel._____

Psychologists
Name_____ Tel._____
Name_____ Tel._____

Psychiatrists
Name_____ Tel._____
Name_____ Tel._____

School-Based Services
Name_____ Tel._____
Name_____ Tel._____

Social Services
Name_____ Tel._____
Name_____ Tel._____

Transition Houses
Name_____ Tel._____
Name_____ Tel._____

Self-Help Groups (Abusers)
Name_____ Tel._____
Name_____ Tel._____

Self-Help Groups (Victims)
Name_____ Tel._____
Name_____ Tel._____

Notes

Preface

[1]Based on a true story told to Catherine Clark Kroeger.

[2]Under the direction of Winnie Bartel, chair of the Women's Commission of the World Evangelical Fellowship, the International Task Force on Abuse was created. The members are Winnie Bartel (U.S.A., chair), Mary Bassali (Egypt), Esme Bower (South Africa), Janice Crouse (U.S.A.), Margaret Jacobs (Australia), Catherine Clark Kroeger (U.S.A.), Lee Eng Lee (Malaysia), Ksenija Magda (Croatia) , Leela Manasseh (India), Judy Mbugua (Kenya), Gwen McVicker (Canada), Olly Mesach (Indonesia), Nancy Nason-Clark (Canada), Grace Nedelchev (Bulgaria), Sharon Payt (U.S.A.), Holly Sheldon (Singapore), Lucett Thomas (Costa Rica) and Blossom White (Jamaica).

Chapter 1: The Prevalence & Severity of Abuse Against Women

[1]We are using the masculine pronoun to refer to perpetrators or abusers and the feminine pronoun to refer to victims. While we recognize that some men are victims of husband battery and some women are perpetrators of that violence, the data from around the world reveal that the overwhelming majority of victims of spousal violence are women and the overwhelming majority of the perpetrators are male.

[2]Nason-Clark 2000a.

[3]Sent directly to Nancy Nason-Clark by the woman on whose life this story is based.

[4]Told to Nancy Nason-Clark after this woman read some of Nancy's published work.

[5]Miles 2000.

[6]Horton, Wilkins and Wright 1998.

[7]The number of evangelical clergy participating in this project was 343, representing a response rate of 70 percent of those clergy contacted.

[8]Nason-Clark 1997.

[9]Horton and Williamson 1998.

[10]Bowker 1998.

[11]Based on stories told to Leela Manasseh, Women's Commission representative from India on the World Evangelical Fellowship and sent to Nancy Nason-Clark by e-mail.

[12]Information supplied by Leela Manasseh, Indian representative on the World Evan-

gelical Fellowship, Commission of Women's Concerns.

[13]Information supplied by Manasseh.

[14]These statistics refer to physical violence only, where the aggressor is a current or former intimate partner. They do not include verbal abuse, sexual abuse or rape.

[15]World Health Organization, "Violence Against Women Information Pack: A Priority Health Issue," 1997.

[16]Heise 1993.

[17]Ibid.

[18]Sample group was married men reporting on violence against their wife in their current marriage.

[19]See Nason-Clark 1998a for a discussion of the impact of Roman Catholic priests' sexual violation on the life of the parish.

[20]World Health Organization, "Violence Against Women Information Pack," 1997.

[21]Female genital mutilation (FGM) is a form of violence against the girl child that affects her life as an adult woman. It is a traditional cultural practice meant to ensure the self-respect of the girl and her family and to increase her marriage opportunities. According to the World Health Organization ("Violence Against Women Information Pack"), FGM constitutes "all procedures that involve partial or total removal of the external female genitalia or other injury to the female genital organs whether for cultural or any other non-therapeutic reasons" (p. 14).

[22]In a World Health Organization document coproduced with UNICEF (1986), S. Ravidran argues that son preference can lead to physical violence against daughters, higher rates of abortion of female fetuses and the practice of female infanticide.

[23]Cited in World Health Organization, "Violence Against Women Information Pack," 1997.

[24]Straus, Gelles and Steinmetz 1980.

[25]Barling and Rosenbaum 1986.

[26]Goldstein and Rosenbaum 1985.

[27]O'Leary and Curley 1986.

[28]Goodwin 1985; O'Leary and Curley 1986.

[29]Jaffe et al. 1986; cf. *Statistics Canada* 1993.

[30]See Nason-Clark 1997, chap. 1.

[31]Ptacek 1988.

[32]Ptacek 1988:249-50.

[33]Abusive men's expectations are often arbitrary and unspoken, so that a wife feels as if she is walking on eggshells, never being sure what is required of her.

[34]Stacey, Hazlewood and Shupe 1994.

[35]Walker 1988.

[36]Bennett 1995; quote on p. 760.

[37]*Statistics Canada* 1993; Straus, Gelles and Steinmetz 1980; Bennett 1995.

[38]Gelles 1985; Gelles and Straus 1979.

[39]Martin 1981.

[40]Gelles 1985; Sullivan and Rumptz 1994; Martin 1981.

[41]Martin 1981; Walker 1984.

[42]See the articles in Timmins 1995 and Horton and Williamson 1988; Gaddis 1996.

[43]For discussions of the needs of the religious woman, see Nason-Clark 1999; Kroeger and Beck 1998.

[44]Nason-Clark 1997; see also Nason-Clark 1998a
[45]Watts, Ndlovu and Keogh 1997.
[46]Nelson and Zimmerman 1996.
[47]*Statistics Canada* 1993.
[48]World Health Organization, "Violence Against Women Information Pack," 1997.
[49]Ellsberg et al. 1996.
[50]Ellsberg et al. 1996.

Chapter 2: Beginning to Respond
[1]Quoted in Nason-Clark 1988b:57.
[2]Quoted in Nason-Clark 1995:123.
[3]Based on a story that emerged from our focus group research; discussed further in Nason-Clark 2000b.
[4]Clergy interview 373, quoted in Nason-Clark 1997:xii.
[5]Clergy interview 376, quoted in Nason-Clark 2000a.
[6]This story appears in Nason-Clark 1997.
[7]Nason-Clark 1998a.

Chapter 3: Growing in Compassion
[1]This story appears in Nason-Clark 1997:38-39.
[2]Quoted in Nason-Clark 1998:62.
[3]Based on a survivor's account told to Nancy Nason-Clark in the northeastern United States.
[4]Langley 1983.
[5]Based on clergy interview 350 in research conducted by Nason-Clark; see Nason-Clark 1997:101.
[6]See Nason-Clark 1995; 1996; 1997; 1998; 1999.
[7]Beaman 1992.
[8]Fortune 1988; Ptacek 1988.
[9]See Alsdurf and Alsdurf 1988; Bowker 1988.
[10]Dobash and Dobash 1979; Walker 1988; Timmins 1995.
[11]Schüssler Fiorenza and Copeland 1994; Brown and Bohn 1989. See also Horton and Williamson 1988; Bussert 1986; Clarke 1986 for early attempts to sound a wake-up call to churches.
[12]Some limited data are available in Alsdurf and Alsdurf 1988 and Bowker 1988, but they are based on rather limited research samples.
[13]See Nason-Clark 1997:chap. 4.
[14]A large proportion of Canadian clergy have reported that they feel ill-equipped to deal with the issues surrounding wife abuse and other forms of family violence and indicate high interest in further training related to these matters (Nason-Clark 1996; 1999).
[15]For a fuller discussion of wife abuse consult DeKeseredy and MacLeod 1999; Martin 1981.
[16]For a fuller discussion of the impact of religious belief on violence, see Clarke 1986; Strom 1986; McDill and McDill 1991; Horton and Williamson 1988.
[17]See Beaman and Nason-Clark 1999; Fortune 1991; Beaman and Nason-Clark 1997.
[18]For a fuller discussion of shelters, see Timmins 1995; G. Walker 1990.
[19]Terris 1996.

Chapter 4: Steeple to Shelter
[1]This story is based on the practices of a community church in Calgary, Alberta; the quilts are donated to the Sheriff King YWCA facility.
[2]See Whipple 1987; Holden, Watts and Brookshire 1991.
[3]See Beaman-Hall and Nason-Clark 1997; Pagelow and Johnson 1988.
[4]Nason-Clark 1997.
[5]Nason-Clark 2000b.
[6]Comments made during focus group interviews, reported more fully in Nason-Clark 1998:60.
[7]Statistics Canada 1993.
[8]Thorne-Finch 1992; McLeod 1987; G. Walker 1990.
[9]This in part explains why shelters do not advertise their addresses to the public; they want to reduce the risk that an abusive man will come to the transitional house seeking retaliation.
[10]The length of stay allowed at most shelters is thirty to ninety days maximum. In some communities second-stage housing is available for women after they have left a transitional house, usually for twelve months or a maximum of two years.
[11]See Smalley 1996; 1998; Dobson 1995; 1996.
[12]See Brown and Bohn 1989; Copeland 1994; Morris 1998; Strom 1986; Fortune 1988; 1991; McDill and McDill 1991; Nason-Clark 1997.

Chapter 5: Searching the Scriptures
[1]Based on a comment from a student during an after-class conversation with Catherine Clark Kroeger.
[2]Such abuse, of course, is not more appropriate if the perpetrator is a woman.
[3]Briggs 1992.
[4]Ibid.
[5]Moore 1999.
[6]Gerhardt 2000:100.

Chapter 6: Man & Woman
[1]Based on a story disclosed by the victim to Catherine Clark Kroeger.

Chapter 7: Does the Suffering of an Abused Woman Bring Salvation to Her Husband?
[1]Story told to Catherine Clark Kroeger.
[2]Based on a story told to Catherine Clark Kroeger after a lecture by a popular woman speaker.
[3]For the latter, Polybius *Histories* 3.36.6-7; 18.15.40; for *hypotassō* as "to bring under the influence of," see Moulton 1970 s.v.
[4]This view was held even by Christians (Augustine *Epistle* 93.3, 185.21; Council of Toledo 16.5.52.4) If a slave was recalcitrant, progressively severe beatings should be employed to secure the desired result. See Macmullen 1984:65 (including notes).
[5]Justin Martyr *2 Apology* 2.1-9.
[6]Balch 1981:105.
[7]Adams 1994:111.

Chapter 8: A Concern for the Christian Family
[1]Based on a story disclosed by telephone to Catherine Clark Kroeger.
[2]Told to Catherine Clark Kroeger by the child's mother.
[3]Told by the victim to Catherine Clark Kroeger.
[4]Based on a personal conversation with Catherine Clark Kroeger.

Chapter 9: Repentance & Forgiveness
[1]Based on a story disclosed by the victim to Catherine Clark Kroeger.

Chapter 11: Good News for & About Abusers
[1]According to Dr. Elizabeth Gerhardt, the focus of treatment for the perpetrator should be on his abusive behavior and on the safety of the victim.
[2]Based on the victim's story told to Catherine Clark Kroeger.

Chapter 12: The Biblical Option of Divorce
[1]Personal conversation by telephone between the therapist and Catherine Clark Kroeger.
[2]According to the research of Nancy Nason-Clark (1997; 1999), pastors want to be involved in any decision regarding the timetable of the possibility of divorce. In this way clergy feel they are able to judge for themselves whether reconciliation is possible.

Chapter 13: Our Global Responsibility
[1]Lloyd 2000.
[2]Abu-Nasr 2000.
[3]Lundgren 1994:34-35
[4]Ibid., p. 35.

References

Print Sources

Abu-Nasr, Donna. 2000. "Honor Crimes: In Some Cultures, the Price of a Woman's Honor Is Blood." *Cape Cod Times,* July 2, p. C1.

Adams, Carol J. 1994. *Woman-Battering.* Creative Pastoral Care and Counseling Series. Minneapolis: Fortress.

Agger, Inger. 1994. *The Blue Room. Trauma and Testimony Among Refugee Women—A Psycho-social Exploration.* Translated by Mary Bille. London: Zed.

Alvarado-Zaldivar, G., J. Salvador-Moysén, S. Estrada-Martinez and A. Terrones-González. 1998. "Prevalencia de violencia domestica en la ciudad de Durango." *Salud pública de Mexico* 40, no. 6:481-86.

Alsdurf, James, and Phyllis Alsdurf. 1988. "Wife Abuse and Scripture." In *Abuse and Religion: When Praying Isn't Enough,* ed. A. Horton and J. Williamson, pp. 221-28. Lexington, Mass: Heath.

American Medical Association. 1992. "Diagnosis and Treatment Guidelines on Domestic Violence." March. Typescript.

American Medical Association Council on Scientific Affairs. 1992. "Violence Against Women: Relevance for Medical Practitioners." *Journal of the American Medical Association* 267, no. 23.

Bachman, Ronet, and L. E. Saltzman. 1995. *Violence Against Women: Estimates from the Redesigned National Crime Victimization Survey.* NCJ-154348. Washington, D.C.: U.S. Department of Justice, Bureau of Justice Statistics.

Balch, David. 1981. *Let Wives Be Submissive: The Domestic Code in First Peter.* Atlanta: Scholars Press.

Baleta, A. 1999. "Studies Reveal the Extent of Domestic Violence in South Africa." *Lancet* 14, no. 354 (August): 580.

Barling, J., and A. Rosenbaum, 1986. "Work Stressors and Wife Abuse." *Journal of Applied Psychology* 71:346-48.

Beaman, Lori G. 1992. "Negotiating the Options: How a Program for Men Who Batter Negotiates Its Identity in a Network of Community Agencies." M.A. thesis, University of New Brunswick, Fredericton, N.B., Canada.

Beaman, Lori G., and Nancy Nason-Clark. 1999. "Evangelical Women as Activists: Their Response to Violence Against Women." In *Shared Beliefs, Different Lives: Women's Identities in Evangelical Context,* pp. 111-32. St. Louis: Chalice.

Beaman-Hall, Lori G., and Nancy Nason-Clark. 1997. "Partners or Protagonists: Exploring the Relationship Between the Transition House Movement and Conservative Churches." *Affilia: Journal of Women and Social Work* 12, no. 2: 176-96.

Bennett, L. W. 1995. "Substance Abuse and the Domestic Assault of Women." *Social Work* 40:760-61.

Bettencourt, B. Ann, and Norman Miller. 1996. "Gender Differences in Aggression as a Function of Provocation: a Meta-analysis." *Psychological Bulletin* 119, no. 3:422-47.

Bewley, S., and Gillian Mezey. 1997. "Domestic Violence and Pregnancy." *British Medical Journal* 314:1295.

Blanc, Ann K., et al. 1996. *Negotiating Reproductive Outcomes in Uganda,* Kampala: Institute of Statistics and Applied Economics; Calverton, Md.: Macro International.

Bohannon, Judy R., David A. Doser and S. Eugene Lindley. 1995. "Using Couple Data to Determine Domestic Violence Rates: An Attempt to Replicate Previous Work." *Violence and Victims* 10, no. 2:133-41.

Bowker, Lee. 1982. "Battered Women and the Clergy: An Evaluation." *Journal of Pastoral Care,* 1982, 36:226-34.

———. 1988. "Religious Leaders and Their Victims: Services Delivered to One Thousand Battered Women by the Clergy." In *Abuse and Religion: When Praying Isn't Enough,* ed. A. Horton and J. Williamson, pp. 229-34. Lexington, Mass: Heath..

Bradley, Christine. 1988. "Wife-Beating in Papua New Guinea: Is It a Problem?" *Papua New Guinea Medical Journal* 31:257-68.

Briggs, David. 1992. "Catholic Bishops Condemn Wife Abuse." *Boston Globe,* October 30.

Brinkerhoff, Merlin B., and Eugen Lupri. 1988. "Interspousal Violence." *Canadian Journal of Sociology* 13, no. 4:407-34.

British Home Office Research and Planning Unit. 1996. *British Crime Survey.*

Brown, Joanne, and Carol Bohn, eds. 1989. *Christianity, Patriarchy and Abuse: A Feminist Critique.* New York: Pilgrim.

Brown, R. 1996. "Violence in America: The Status Today." American Medical Association, June. Typescript.

Browning, James, and Donald Dutton. 1986. "Assessment of Wife Assault with the Conflict Tactics Scale: Using Couple Data to Quantify the Differential Reporting Effect." *Journal of Marriage and the Family* 48:375-79.

Brush, L. 1990. "Violent Acts and Injurious Outcomes in Married Couples: Methodological Issues in the National Survey of Family and Households." *Gender and Society* 4, no. 1:56-67.

Burbank, Victoria K. 1987. "Female Aggression in Cross-cultural Perspective." *Behavior Science Research* 21:70-100.

Bussert, J. M. K. 1986. *Battered Women: From a Theology of Suffering to an Ethic of Empowerment.* New York: Lutheran Church of America, Division for Mission in North America.

Cantos, Arthur L., Peter H. Neidig and K. Daniel O'Leary. 1994. "Injuries of Women and Men in a Treatment Program for Domestic Violence." *Journal of Family Violence* 9, no. 2:113-24.

Carrillo, R. 1992. *Battered Dreams: Violence Against Women as an Obstacle to Development.* New York: United Nations Fund for Women.

Carlson, Bonnie E. 1984. "Children's Observations of Interparental Violence." In *Battered Women and Their Families: Intervention Strategies and Treatment Programs,* ed. Albert R. Roberts, pp. 147-67. New York: Springer.

Centro Paraguayo de Estudios de Población. 1996. *Encuesta nacional de demografía y salud reproductiva, 1995-1996.* Paraguay: Centro Paraguayo de Estudios de Población.

Christian Reformed Church Committee to Study Physical, Emotional and Sexual Abuse. 1992. "Report 30." In *The Agenda for Synod 1992 of the Christian Reformed Church in North America,* pp. 313-58. Grand Rapids, Mich.: CRC Publications.

Clarke, Rita-Lou. 1986. *Pastoral Care of Battered Women.* Philadelphia: Westminster Press.

Clinkin, C. 1994. "Rape and Sexual Abuse of Women in International Law." *European Journal of International Law* 326:23-28.

Colombia Demographic Health Surveys (DHS) III. 1995. *Encuesta national de demografía y salud, 1995.* Bogotá: Profamilia; Calverton, Md.: Macro International.

Commonwealth Secretariat. 1992. *Confronting Violence: A Manual for Commonwealth Action.* London: Women and Development Programme, Commonwealth Secretariat.

Cook, Rebecca J., ed. 1994. *Human Rights of Women: National and International Perspectives.* Philadelphia: University of Pennsylvania Press.

Copeland, Mary Shawn. 1994. "Reflections." In *Violence Against Women,* ed. Elisabeth Schüssler Fiorenza and M. S. Copeland, pp. 119-22. London: SCM Press.

Cosgrove, Katie. "No Man Has the Right." 1996. In *Women in a Violent World: Feminist Analyses and Resistance Across "Europe,"* ed. Chris Corrin. Edinburgh: Edinburgh University Press.

Dan, Alice J., ed. 1994. *Reframing Women's Health: Multi-disciplinary Research and Practice.* Thousand Oaks, Calif.: Sage.

Davies, Miranda, ed. 1994. *Women and Violence: Realities and Responses Worldwide.* London: Zed.

DeKeseredy, Walter S. 1992. "In Defense of Self-Defense: Demystifying Female Violence Against Male Intimates." In *Debates in Canadian Society,* ed. R. Hinch, pp. 245-52. Toronto: Nelson.

———. 1995. "Enhancing the Quality of Survey Data on Woman Abuse." *Violence Against Women* 1, no. 2:158-73.

DeKeseredy, Walter S., and Brian D. Maclean. 1990. "Researching Woman Abuse in Canada: A Realistic Critique of the Conflict Tactics Scale." *Canadian Review of Social Policy* 25:19-27.

DeKeseredy, Walter S., and Linda MacLeod. 1998. *Woman Abuse: A Sociological Story.* Toronto: Harcourt Brace.

DeKeseredy, Walter S., D. G. Saunders, M. D. Schwartz, and S. Alvi. 1997. "The Meanings and Motives for Women's Use of Violence in Canadian College Dating Relationships: Results from a National Survey." *Sociological Spectrum* 17:199-222.

Demographic and Health Surveys (DHS). 1994. "Domestic Violence and Rape." In *National Safe Motherhood Survey, 1993.* Calverton, Md.: Macro International.

Departamento de Salud y Escuela de Salud Pública and Centers for Disease Control and Prevention. 1998. *Encuesto de salud reproductiva 1995-1996: Resumen de los hallazgos.* San Juan: Universidad de Puerto Rico/CDC.

Deyessa, N., et al. 1998. "Magnitude, Type and Outcomes of Physical Violence Against Married Women in Butajira, Southern Ethiopia." *Ethiopian Medical Journal* 36:83-92.

Dobash, R. P., and R. E. Dobash. 1979. *Violence Against Wives: A Case Against the Patriarchy.* New York: Free Press.

———. 1983. "Patterns of Violence in Scotland." In *International Perspectives on Family*

Violence, ed. R. Gelles and C. Cornell. Lexington, Mass.: Lexington.

————. 1995. "Domestic Violence: The Northern Ireland Response." In *Women and Violence,* ed. M. Davies. London: Zed.

Dobash, R. P., et al. 1998. "Separate and Intersecting Realities: A Comparison of Men's and Women's Accounts of Violence Against Women." *Journal of Violence Against Women* 4, no. 4:382-414.

Dobson, James C. 1995. *Straight Talk: What Men Need to Know; What Women Should Understand.* Dallas: Word.

————. 1996. *Love Must Be Tough: New Hope for Families in Crisis.* Dallas: Word.

Dutton, Donald. G., and Kenneth J. Hemphill. 1992. "Patterns of Socially Desirable Responding Among Perpetrators and Victims of Wife Assault." *Violence and Victims* 7, no. 1:29-39.

Ellsberg, Mary Carroll. 1997. *Candies in Hell: Domestic Violence Against Women in Nicaragua.* Umea, Sweden: Department of Epidemiology and Public Health, Umea University.

Ellsberg, Mary Carroll, et al. 1996. *Confites en el infierno: Prevalencia y características de la violencia conyugal hacia las mujeres en Nicaragua.* Managua: Asociación de Mujeres Profesionales por la Democracia en el Desarrollo.

Elman, R., and M. Eduards. 1991. "Unprotected by the Swedish Welfare State: A Survey of Battered Women and the Assistance They Received." *Women's Studies International Forum* 14, no. 5:413-21.

El-Zanaty, F., et al. 1996. *Egypt Demographic and Health Surveys III.* Cairo: National Population Council; Calverton, Md.: Macro International.

Falik, Marilyn M., and Karen Scott Collins, eds. 1996. *Women's Health: The Commonwealth Fund Survey.* Baltimore, Md.: Johns Hopkins University Press.

Family Violence Prevention Fund. 1993. "Men Beating Women: Ending Domestic Violence—A Qualitative and Quantitative Study of Public Attitudes on Violence Against Women." New York: EDK Associates.

Federal Bureau of Investigation. 1988. "Supplement Homicide Report from the Uniform Crime Reports and a Bureau of Justice Statistics Study." Washington, D.C. Annual report.

————. 1992. "Uniform Crime Reports: Crime for the United States." Washington, D.C. Annual report.

Fennell, Caroline. 1993. "Criminal Law and the Criminal Justice System: Woman as Victim." In *Gender and Law in Ireland,* ed. A. Connelly. Dublin: Oak Tree.

Finkelhor, David, et al., eds. 1983. *The Dark Side of Families: Current Family Violence Research.* Beverly Hills, Calif.: Sage.

Foley, M. 1995. " 'Who Is in Control?' Changing Responses to Women Who Have Been Raped and Sexually Abused." In *Women, Violence and Male Power: Feminist Activism, Research and Practice,* ed. Marianne Hester, Liz Kelly, and Jill Radford. Milton Keynes, England: Open University Press.

Fortune, Marie. 1987. *Keeping the Faith: Questions and Answers for the Abused Woman.* San Francisco: Harper.

————. 1988. "Reporting Child Abuse: An Ethical Mandate for Ministry." In *Abuse and Religion: When Praying Isn't Enough,* ed. A. Horton and J. Williamson, pp. 189-98. Lexington, Mass.: Heath.

————. 1991. *Violence in the Family: A Workshop Curriculum for Clergy and Other Helpers.*

Cleveland, Ohio: Pilgrim.

————. 1998. "Preaching Forgiveness?" In *Telling the Truth: Preaching about Sexual and Domestic Violence*, ed. John S. McClure and Nancy J. Ramsay, pp. 49-57. Cleveland, Ohio: United Church Press.

Gaddis, Patricia Riddle. 1996. *Battered but Not Broken: Help for Abused Wives and Their Church Families*. Valley Forge, Penn.: Judson.

Gelles, Richard J. 1985. "Family Violence." *Annual Review of Sociology* 11:347-67.

Gelles, Richard J., and Murray A. Straus. 1979. "Violence in the American Family." *Journal of Social Issues* 35:15-39.

Gelles, Richard J., and Donileen R. Loseke, eds. 1993. *Current Controversies on Family Violence*. Newbury Park, Calif.: Sage.

Gerhardt, Elizabeth L. 2000. "Martin Luther's Theology of the Cross: Cause or Cure of Domestic Violence?" Th.D. diss., Boston University.

Gill, M., and Leslie M. Tutty. 1997. "Sexual Identity Issues for Male Survivors of Childhood Sexual Abuse: A Qualitative Study." *Journal of Child Sexual Abuse* 6, no. 3:31-47.

Gillioz, L., et al. 1996. *"Domination masculine et violences envers les femmes dans la famille en Suisse."* Typescript, Geneva.

Gillioz, L., et al. 1997. *Domination et violences envers les femmes dans la couple*. Lausanne: Editions Payot.

Goldstein, D., and A. Rosenbaum. 1985. "An Evaluation of the Self Esteem of Maritally Violent Men." *Family Relations* 34:425-28.

Gonzales de Olarte, E., et al. 1997. *Poverty and Domestic Violence Against Women in Metropolitan Lima*. Washington, D.C.: Inter-American Development Bank.

Goodwin, J. 1985. "Family Violence: Principles of Intervention and Prevention." *Hospital and Community Psychiatry* 36:1074-79.

Grandin, Elaine, and Eugen Lupri. 1997. "Intimate Violence in Canada and the United States: A Cross-national Comparison." *Journal of Family Violence* 12, no. 4:417-43.

Guiliani, M. 1991. "Battered Women." *New Directions for Women* 20, no. 2: 4.

Haj-Yahia, Muhammad M. 1997. "The First National Survey of Abuse and Battering Against Arab Women from Israel: Preliminary Results." Typescript.

————. 1998. *The Incidence of Wife-Abuse and Battering and Some Sociodemographic Correlates as Revealed in Two National Surveys in Palestinian Society*. Ramallah, Palestinian Authority: Besir Center for Research and Development.

Hamby, S. L., Valerie C. Pondexter and Bernadette Gray-Little. 1996. "Four Measures of Partner Violence: Construct Similarity and Classification Differences." *Journal of Marriage and the Family* 58:127-39.

Heise, Lori. 1993. "Violence Against Women: The Hidden Health Burden." *World Health Statistical Quarterly* 46, no. 1:78-85.

Heise, Lori, Jacqueline Pitanguy and Adrienne Germain. 1994. *Violence Against Women: The Hidden Health Burden*. World Bank Discussion Paper 255. Washington, D.C.: World Bank.

Heise, Lori, et al. 1994. "Violence Against Women: A Neglected Public Health Issue in Less Developed Countries." *Social Science and Medicine* 39, no. 4:1165-79.

Hoffman, Kristi, et al. 1994. "Physical Wife Abuse in a Non-Western Society: An Integrated Theoretical Approach." *Journal of Marriage and the Family* 56:131-46.

Holden, Janice Miner, R. E. Watts and W. Brookshire. 1991. "Beliefs of Professional

Counselors and Clergy About Depressive Religious Ideation." *Counseling and Values* 35:93-103.

Horton, Anne, Melany Wilkins, and Wendy Wright. 1988. "Women Who Ended Abuse: What Religious Leaders and Religion Did for These Victims." In *Abuse and Religion: When Praying Isn't Enough*, ed. A. Horton and J. Williamson, pp. 235-46. Lexington, Mass: Heath.

Horton, Anne, and Judith Williamson, eds. 1988. *Abuse and Religion: When Praying Isn't Enough*. Lexington, Mass.: Heath.

Ilkkaracan, Pinar, and Women for Women's Human Rights. 1988. "Exploring the Context of Women's Sexuality in Eastern Turkey." *Reproductive Health Matters* 6, no. 12:66-75.

———. 1997. "Domestic Violence and Family Life as Experienced by Turkish Immigrant Women in Germany." Report 3. Istanbul: Women for Women's Human Rights.

Jacobson, N. S., et al. 1994. "Affect, Verbal Content and Psychophysiology in the Arguments of Couples with a Violent Husband." *Journal of Consulting and Clinical Psychology* 62, no. 5:982-88.

Jaffe, Peter, et al. 1986. "Similarities in Behavioral and Social Maladjustment Among Child Victims and Witnesses to Family Violence." *American Journal of Orthopsychiatry* 56, no. 1:142-46.

Jejeebhoy, Shireen, and Rebecca J. Cook. 1997. "State Accountability for Wife-Beating: The Indian Challenge." *Lancet* 348 (supp.): sl10-sl12.

Jewkes, R., et al. 1999. " 'He Must Give Me Money, He Mustn't Beat Me': Violence Against Women in Three South African Provinces." Pretoria: Medical Research Council. Typescript.

Johnson, Michael P. 1995. "Patriarchal Terrorism and Common Couple Violence: Two Forms of Violence Against Women." *Journal of Marriage and the Family* 57:283-94.

Jurevic, Linda S. 1996. "Between a Rock and a Hard Place: Women Victims of Domestic Violence and the Western Australian Criminal Injuries Compensation Act." *Murdoch University Electronic Journal of Law* 3, no. 2 (July).

Kerr, J., ed. 1994. *Calling for Change: International Strategies to End Violence Against Women*. The Hague: Development Cooperation Information Department, Ministry of Foreign Affairs.

Khodyreva, Natalia. 1996. "Sexism and Sexual Abuse in Russia." In *Women in a Violent World: Feminist Analyses and Resistance Across "Europe,"* ed. Chris Corrin. Edinburgh: Edinburgh University Press.

Kim, K., and Y. Cho. 1992. "Epidemiological Survey of Spousal Abuse in Korea." In *Intimate Violence: Interdisciplinary Perspectives*, ed. Emilio Viano. Washington, D.C.: Hemisphere.

Koss, Mary P., et al. 1991. "Deleterious Effects of Criminal Victimisation on Women's Health and Medical Utilisation." *Archives of Internal Medicine* 151:342-47.

Kroeger, Catherine Clark, and James Beck, eds. 1998. *Healing the Hurting: Giving Hope and Help to Abused Women*. Grand Rapids, Mich.: Baker.

Langhinrichsen-Rohling, Jennifer, Peter Neidig and George Thorn. 1995. "Violent Marriages: Gender Differences in Level of Current Violence and Past Abuse." *Journal of Family Violence* 10, no. 2:159-76.

Langley, Myrtle. 1983. *Equal Woman: A Christian Feminist Perspective*. Basingstoke, U.K.:

Marshall, Morgan & Scott.

Larrain, Soledad. 1993. *Estudio de frecuencia de la violencia intrafamiliar y la condición de la mujer en Chile.* Santiago: Pan American Health Organisation.

Larrain-Heiremans, S. 1993. "Violencia familiar y la situacion de la mujer en Chile." Typescript.

Latin American and Caribbean Women's Health Network. 1996. *The Right to Live Without Violence: The Women's Health Collection.* Santiago: Women's Health Network.

Leonard, M. 1993. "Rape: Myths and Reality." In *Irish Women's Studies Reader,* ed. Alibhe Smyth. Dublin: Attic.

Leung, W. C., et al. 1999. "The Prevalence of Domestic Violence Against Pregnant Women in a Chinese Community." *International Journal of Gynecology and Obstetrics* 6, no. 1 (July): 23-30.

Lieberman Research. 1995. "Domestic Violence Advertising Campaign Tracking Survey: Wave III, November 1995." San Francisco: The Advertising Council and Family Violence Prevention Fund. Typescript.

Lloyd, Marion. 2000. "To Prevent Dowry-Related Slayings, Women Urge India to Revamp Laws." *Boston Globe,* June 23, p. 2.

Louis, M-V. 1994. "Sexual Harassment at Work in France: What Stakes for Feminists?" In *Women and Violence: Realities and Responses Worldwide,* ed. Miranda Davies. London: Zed.

Lundgren, Eva. 1994. " 'I Am Endowed with All the Power in Heaven and on Earth': When Men Become Men Through 'Christian' Abuse," *Studia Theologica: Scandinavian Journal of Theology.* 48, no. 1.

Lung, C. T., and D. Daro. 1996. *Current Trends in Child Abuse Reporting Fatalities: The Results of the 1995 Annual Fifty State Survey.* Chicago: National Committee to Prevent Child Abuse.

Macmullen, Ramsay. 1984. *Christianizing the Roman Empire A.D. 100-400.* New Haven, Conn.: Yale University Press.

Mama, Amina. 1989. "Violence Against Black Women: Gender, Race and State Response." *Feminist Review* 32:30-48.

———. 1990. "A Hidden Struggle: Black Women and Violence." *Spare Rib* 209 (February): 8-11.

———. 1993. "Woman Abuse in London's Black Communities." In *Inside Babylon: The Caribbean Diaspora in Britain,* ed. W. James and C. Harris. London: Verso.

Marin, L., H. Zia and E. Soler, eds. 1998. *Ending Domestic Violence: Report from the Global Frontlines.* San Francisco: Family Violence Prevention Fund.

Martin, Del. 1981. *Battered Wives.* San Francisco: New Glide.

Maynard, Mary, and Jan Winn. 1993. "Violence Towards Women." In *Introducing Women's Studies,* ed. Diane Richardson and Victoria Robinson. London: Macmillan.

Mazza, D., et al. 1996. "Physical, Sexual and Emotional Violence Against Women: A General Practice-Based Prevalence Study." *Medical Journal of Australia* 164, no. 1:14-17.

McDill, S. R., and Linda McDill. 1991. *Shattered and Broken: Wife Abuse in the Christian Community: Guidelines for Hope and Healing.* Old Tappan, N.J.: Revell.

McFarlane, Judith, et al. 1991. "Assessing for Abuse: Self-Report Versus Nurse Interview." *Public Health Nursing* 8, no. 4:245-50.

McLeod, Linda. 1987. *Battered but Not Beaten: Preventing Wife Battering in Canada.*

Ottawa: Canadian Advisory Council on the Status of Women.

Mezey, G. C., and S. Bewley. 1997. "Domestic Violence and Pregnancy." *British Medical Journal* (British Medical Association) 314, no. 7090 (May 3): 1295.

Miles, Al. 2000. *Domestic Violence: What Every Pastor Needs to Know.* Minneapolis: Augsburg Fortress.

Miller, G. 1989. "Violence by and Against America's Children." *Journal of Juvenile Justice Digest* 17, no. 12:6.

Mirrlees-Black, Catriona, Pat Mayhew, and Andrew Percy. 1996. "The 1996 British Crime Survey, England and Wales." *Home Office Statistical Bulletin* 19, no. 96.

Mooney, J. 1993. *The Hidden Figure: Domestic Violence in North London.* London: School of Sociology and Social Policy, Middlesex University.

Moore, Sheila Y. 1999. "Adolescent Boys Are the Underserved Victims of Domestic Violence." *Boston Globe,* December 26, p. E7.

Morley, Rebecca. 1993. "Recent Responses to Domestic Violence Against Women: A Feminist Critique." In *Social Policy Review 5: The Evolving State of Welfare,* ed. R. Page and J. Baldock. Canterbury: Social Policy Association.

Morris, R. 1988. *Ending Violence Against Families: A Training Program for Pastoral Care Workers,* Toronto: United Church of Canada.

Morrison, Andrew, and Maria Beatring Orlando. 1997. *The Socio-economic Impact of Domestic Violence Against Women in Chile and Nicaragua.* Washington, D.C.: Inter-American Development Bank.

Morse, Barbara J. 1995. "Beyond the Conflict Tactics Scale: Assessing Differences in Partner Violence." *Violence and Victims* 10, no. 4:251-72.

Moulton, Harold. 1970. *Analytical Greek Lexicon.* Grand Rapids, Mich.: Zondervan.

Mullen, P., et al. 1988. "Impact of Sexual and Physical Abuse on Women's Mental Health." *Lancet* 1:841-45.

Myers, J. A. 1994. "Advocates Versus Researchers—A False Dichotomy? A Feminist, Social Constructionist Response to Jacobson." *Family Process* 33:87-91.

Narayana, G. 1996. "Family Violence, Sex and Reproductive Health Behaviour Among Men in Uttar Pradesh, India." Paper presented at the annual meeting of the National Council on International Health, Arlington, Va., June. ·

Nason-Clark, Nancy. 1995. "Conservative Protestants and Violence Against Women: Exploring the Rhetoric and the Response." In Mary Jo Neitz and Marion Goldman, eds. *Sex, Lies and Sanctity: Deviance and Religion in Contemporary America,* Greenwich, Conn.: JAI, 1995, pp.109-30.

——. 1996. "Religion and Violence Against Women: Exploring the Rhetoric and the Response of Evangelical Churches in Canada." *Social Compass,* 46, no. 4:515-536.

——. 1997. *The Battered Wife: How Christians Confront Family Violence.* Louisville, Ky.: Westminster John Knox.

——. 1998a. "Abuses of Clergy Trust: Exploring the Impact on Female Congregants' Faith and Practice." In *Wolves Among the Fold,* ed. Anson Shupe, pp. 85-100. New York: Rutgers University Press.

——. 1998b. "Canadian Evangelical Church Women and Responses to Family Violence." In *Religion in a Changing World: Comparative Studies in Sociology,* ed. Madeleine Cousineau. Westport, Conn.: Greenwood.

——. 1998c. "The Evangelical Family Is Sacred . . But Is It Safe?" In *Healing the Hurting: Giving Hope and Help to Abused Women,* ed. Catherine Clark Kroeger and

James R. Beck. Grand Rapids, Mich.: Baker.

———. 2000a. "Defining violence in religious contexts." In *Bad Pastors: Clergy Malfeasance in America*, ed. Anson Shupe. Albany: New York University Press, 2000.

———. 2000b. "Religion, Violence and Social Welfare." In *Religion and Social Policy for the Twenty-first Century*, ed. P. Nesbitt. Walnut Creek, Calif.: AltaMira.

———. 2000c. "Shattered Silence or Holy Hush: Emerging Definitions of Violence Against Women." *Journal of Family Ministry* 13, no. 1:39-56.

National Health and Social Survey. In *Sex in America: A Definitive Survey*, ed. R. T. Micheal et al., pp. 40-44. New York: National Academic Press.

National Violence Against Women Survey. 1998. Washington, D.C.: National Institute of Justice; Atlanta: Centers for Disease Control and Prevention, November.

Nelson, Erin, and Cathy Zimmerman. 1996. *Household Survey on Domestic Violence in Cambodia*. Phnom Penh: Cambodia Ministry of Women's Affairs, Project Against Domestic Violence.

Nordquist, J. 1998. *Violence Against women—International Aspects: A Bibliography*. Contemporary Social Issues: A Bibliographic Series 49. Santa Cruz, Calif.: Reference and Research Services.

Odujinrin, O. 1993. "Wife Battering in Nigeria." *International Journal of Gynecology and Obstetrics* 41:159-64.

O'Leary, K. D., and A. D. Curley. 1986. "Assertion and Family Violence: Correlates of Spouse Abuse." *Journal of Marital and Family Therapy* 12:281-89.

O'Leary, K. D., et al. 1989. "Prevalence and Stability of Physical Aggression Between Spouses: A Longitudinal Analysis." *Journal of Consulting and Clinical Psychology* 57, no. 2:263-68.

Pagelow, M. D., and P. Johnson. 1988. "Abuse in the American Family: The Role of Religion." In *Abuse and Religion: When Praying Isn't Enough*, ed. A. Horton and J. Williamson, pp. 1-12. Lexington, Mass.: Heath.

Peled, I., P. G. Jaffe and J.L. Edleson, eds. 1995. *Ending the Cycle of Violence: Community Responses to Children of Battered Women*. Thousand Oaks, Calif.: Sage.

Peters, J. S., and Andrea Wolper, eds. 1995. *Women's Rights, Human Rights: International Feminist Perspectives*. New York: Routledge.

Plichta, S. B., et al. 1992. "The Effects of Woman Abuse on Health Care Utilisation and Health Status: A Literature Review." *Women's Health Issues* 2, no. 3:154-61.

———. 1996. "Violence and Gynaecologic Health in Women <50 years old." *American Journal of Obstetrics and Gynecology* 174:903-7.

ProFamilia. 1990. *Encuesta de prevalencia, demografía y salud* (Demographic and Health Survey). Bogotá: Profamilia; Calverton, Md.: Macro International.

Ptacek, James. 1988. "How Men Who Batter Rationalize Their Behavior." In *Abuse and Religion: When Praying Isn't Enough*, ed. A. Horton and J. Williamson, pp. 247-58. Lexington, Mass.: Heath.

Radford, Jill, and Elizabeth Stanko. 1995. "Violence Against Women and Children: The Contradictions of Crime Control Under Patriarchy." In *Women, Violence and Male Power: Feminist Activism, Research and Practice*, ed. Marianne Hester, Liz Kelly, and Jill Redford, pp. 65-80. Milton Keynes, England: Open University Press. First published in *The Politics of Crime Control*, ed. Kevin Stenson and David Cowell. London: Sage, 1991.

Raikes, Alanagh. 1990. *Pregnancy, Birthing and Family Planning in Kenya—Changing Pat-*

terns of Behaviour: A Health Utilisation Study in Kissi District. Copenhagen: Centre for Development Research.

Ramirez Rodriguez, Juan Carlos, et al. 1996. "Una espada de doble filo: La salud reproductiva y la violencia doméstica contra la mujer." Presentation to Seminario Salud Reproductiva en America Latina y el Caribe, Brazil.

Randall, Margaret, and L. Haskell. 1995. "Sexual Violence in Women's Lives: Findings from the Women's Safety Project, a Community-Based Survey." *Violence Against Women* 1, no. 1 (March): 6-31.

Rodgers, K. 1994. "Wife Assault: The Findings of a National Survey." *Juristat Service Bulletin of the Canadian Centre for Justice Statistics* 14, no. 9:1-22.

Rodríguez, J., and P. Becerra. 1997. "Que tan serio es el problema de la violencia doméstica contra la mujer? Algunos datos para la discusión." Paper presented at the Congreso Nacional de Investigación en Salud Pública, Brazil. March.

Römkens, Renée. 1997. "Prevalence of Wife Abuse in the Netherlands: Combining Quantitative and Qualitative Methods in Survey Research." *Journal of Interpersonal Violence* 12. no. 1:99-125.

Rothenberg, Karen H., et al. 1995. "Domestic Violence and Partner Notification: Implications for Treatment and Counseling of Women with HIV." *Journal of the American Medical Women's Association* 50, no. 3:87-93.

Rothery, M., L. Tutty and G. Weaver. 1999. "Tough Choices: Women, Abusive Partners and the Ecology of Decision-Making." *Canadian Journal of Community Mental Health*, spring.

Saltzman, L. 1995. "Violence Against Women Estimated from the Redesigned Survey," National Crime Victimization Survey, U.S. Department of Justice, Bureau of Justice Statistics, August monthly report.

Saunders, Daniel G. 1986. "When Battered Women Use Violence: Husband-Abuse or Self-Defense?" *Victims and Violence* 1, no. 1:47-60.

Schafer, J. Raul Caetano and Catherine L. Clark. 1998. "Rates of Intimate Partner Violence in the United States." *American Journal of Public Health* 88, no. 11:1702-4.

Schei, Berit, and L. S. Bakketeig. 1989. "Gynaecological Impact of Sexual and Physical Abuse by Spouse: A Study of a Random Sample of Norwegian Women." *British Journal of Obstetrics and Gynaecology* 96:1379-83.

Schuler, Sidney Ruth, et al. 1996. "Credit Programs, Patriarchy and Men's Violence Against Women in Rural Bangladesh." *Social Science and Medicine* 43, no. 12:1729-42.

Schüssler Fiorenza, Elisabeth, and M. S. Copeland, eds. 1994. *Violence Against Women*. London: SCM Press.

Schwartz, M. D. 1987. "Gender and Injury in Spousal Assault." *Sociological Focus* 20, no. 1:61-75.

Seager, Joni. 1997. *The State of Women in the World Atlas*. New ed. London: Penguin.

Sexwale, B. 1994. "Violence Against Women: Experiences of South African Domestic Workers." In *The Dynamic of "Race" and Gender: Some Feminist Interventions*, ed. Haleh Afshar and Mary Maynard. Bristol, Penn.: Taylor & Francis.

Shaw, M. 1996. "The Survey of Federally Sentenced Women, as Cited in *The Arbour Report*." Ottawa: Correctional Services of Canada.

Shelly, L. 1987. "Inter-personal Violence in the USSR." *Violence, Aggression and Terrorism* 1, no. 2:41-67

Shiroma, M. 1996. *Salud reproductiva y violencia contra la mujer: Un análisis desde la perspec-*

tiva ∂e género. Nuevo León: Asociación Mexicana de Población, Consejo Estatal de Población, Colegio de México.

Siddiqui, Hannana. 1996. "Domestic Violence in Asian Communities: The Experience of Southall Black Sisters." In *Women in a Violent Worl∂: Feminist Analyses an∂ Resistance Across "Europe,"* ed. Chris Corrin. Edinburgh: Edinburgh University Press.

Siklova, J., and J. Hradilkova. 1994. "Women and Violence in Post-Communist Czechoslovakia." In *Women an∂ Violence,* ed. Miranda Davies. London: Zed.

Smalley, Gary. 1988. *Hi∂∂en Keys of a Loving, Lasting Marriage,* Grand Rapids, Mich.: Zondervan.

————. 1996. *Making Love Last Forever.* Dallas: Word.

Smyth, Ailbhe. 1996. "Seeing Red: Men's Violence Against Women in Ireland." In *Women in a Violent Worl∂: Feminist Analyses an∂ Resistance Across "Europe,"* ed. Chris Corrin. Edinburgh: Edinburgh University Press.

South Africa Department of Health. 1999. *South Africa Demographic an∂ Health Survey, 1988: Preliminary Report.* Calverton, Md.: Macro International.

Spijkerboer, Thomas. 1994. *Women an∂ Refugee Status: Beyon∂ the Public/Private Distinction.* The Hague: Emancipation Council, September.

Stacey, William, Lonnie Hazlewood and Anson Shupe. 1994. *The Violent Couple.* New York: Praeger.

Stacey, William L., and Anson Shupe. 1983. *The Family Secret.* Boston: Beacon, 1983.

Stanko, B. 1995. "The Struggle over Common Sense: Feminism, Violence and Confronting the Backlash." In *Procee∂ings of the Fifth Symposium on Violence an∂ Aggression,* ed. B. Gillis and G. James, pp. 156-72. Saskatoon: University of Saskatchewan Press.

Stark, Evan, and Anne Flitcraft. 1982. "Medical Therapy as Repression: The Case of Battered Women." *Health an∂ Me∂icine,* summer-fall, pp. 29-32.

Statistics Canada. 1993. *The Violence Against Women Survey. The Daily,* November 18.

Straus, Murray A., and Richard J. Gelles. 1986. "Societal Change and Change in Family Violence from 1975 to 1985 as Revealed by Two National Surveys." *Journal of Marriage an∂ the Family* 48 (August): 465-79.

————, eds. 1990. *Physical Violence in American Families: Risk Factors an∂ A∂aptations to Violence in 8,145 Families.* New Brunswick, N.J.: Transaction.

Straus, Murray A., Richard J. Gelles, and Susan K. Steinmetz. 1980. *Behin∂ Close∂ Doors: Violence in the American Family.* Garden City, N.Y.: Doubleday/Anchor.

Strom, Kay Marshall. 1986. *In the Name of Submission.* Portland, Ore.: Multnomah Press.

Sullivan, C. M., and M. H. Rumptz. 1994. "Adjustment and Needs of African-American Women Who Utilized a Domestic Violence Shelter." *Violence an∂ Victims* 9:275-86.

Swiss, S., and J. Giller. 1993. "Rape as a Crime of War: A Medical Perspective." *Journal of the American Me∂ical Association* 270:612-15.

Szinovacz, Maximiliane E., and Lance C. Egley. 1995. "Comparing One-Partner and Couple Data on Sensitive Marital Behaviors: The Case of Marital Violence." *Journal of Marriage an∂ the Family* 57:1995-2020.

Terris, Christy. 1996. "Cares, Conflict and Counselling: A Study of Evangelical Youth and Their Youth Pastors." M.A. thesis, University of New Brunswick, Fredericton.

Thorne-Finch, Ron. 1992. *En∂ing the Silence: The Origins an∂ Treatment of Male Violence*

Against Women. Toronto: University of Toronto Press.

Timmins, Leslie. 1995. *Listening to the Thunder: Advocates Talk About the Battered Women's Movement.* Vancouver, B.C.: Women's Research Centre.

Trainor, C. 1999. "Canada's Shelters for Abused Women." *Juristat Bulletin of the Canadian Centre for Justice Statistics* 19 no. 6.

Tutty, Leslie M. 1998. "Mental Health Issues of Abused Women: The Perceptions of Shelter Workers." *Canadian Journal of Community Mental Health,* spring.

Tutty, Leslie M., et al. Forthcoming. "An Evaluation of Men's Batterer Treatment Groups." *Research on Social Work Practice.*

United Nations. 1989. *Violence Against Women in the Family.* New York: United Nations.

———. 1994a. "Declaration on the Elimination of Violence Against Women." Resolution No. A/Res/48/104. New York: United Nations, February 23.

———. 1994b. "Preliminary Report of the Special Rapporteur on Violence Against Women, Its Causes and Consequences in Accordance with Commission on Human Rights Resolution 1994/45." Document E/CN.4/1995/42. New York: Economic and Social Council, Commission on Human Rights.

———. 1994c. *Strategies for Confronting Domestic Violence: A Resource Manual.* New York: United Nations.

———. 1995. "The World's Women 1995: Trends and Statistics." *Social Statistics and Indicators,* series K, no. 12.

———. 1996. "Report of the Special Rapporteur on Violence Against Women, Its Causes and Consequences, in Accordance with Commission on Human Rights Resolution 1995/85." Document E/CN.4/1996/53. New York: Economic and Social Council, Commission on Human Rights.

———. 1997. "Report of the Special Rapporteur on Violence Against Women, Its Causes and Its Consequences." Document E/CN.4/1997/47. New York: Economic and Social Council, Commission on Human Rights.

———. 1998. "Status of Women Commission Hears Call for Elaboration of Legally Binding International Instrument on Violence Against Women." Status of Women Press Release, March 5.

United States Department of Justice. 1993. "National Crime Victimization Survey, 1973-92." Washington, D.C.: Bureau of Justice Statistics.

———. 1995. "National Crime Victimization Survey, 1992-93." Washington, D.C.: Bureau of Justice Statistics, August.

———. 1998. *Prevalence, Incidence and Consequences of Violence Against Women: Findings from the National Violence Against Women Survey.* Washington, D.C.: Department of Justice.

van der Straten, A. 1995. "Couple Communication, Sexual Coercion and HIV Risk Reduction in Kigali, Rwanda." *AIDS* 9, no. 8:935-44.

Vivian, D., and Jennifer Langhinrichsen-Rohling. 1994. "Are Bi-directionally-Violent Couples Mutually Victimized? A Gender-Sensitive Comparison." *Violence and Victims* 9, no. 2:107-24.

Walker, Lenore. 1988. "Spouse Abuse: A Basic Profile." In *Abuse and Religion: When Praying Isn't Enough,* ed. Anne Horton and Judith Williamson, pp. 13-20. Lexington, Mass.: Heath.

Walker, Gillian. 1984. *The Battered Woman Syndrome.* New York: Springer.

———. 1990. *Family Violence and the Women's Movement: The Conceptual Politics of Struggle.*

Toronto: University of Toronto Press.

Watts, C., M. Ndlovu, and E. Keogh. 1997. *The Magnitude and Health Consequences of Violence Against Women in Zimbabwe: Musasa Project Report, 1997.* Geneva: World Health Organization, July.

Whipple, Vicky. 1987. "Counseling Battered Women from Fundamendalist Churches." *Journal for Marital and Family Therapy* 13, no. 3:251-58.

White, J. W., and Robin M. Kowalski. 1994. "Deconstructing the Myth of the Nonaggressive Woman." *Psychology of Women Quarterly* 18: 487-508.

Wilson, M., and Martin Daly. 1993. "Spousal Homicide Risk and Estrangement." *Victims and Violence* 8, no. 1:3-16.

———. 1994. "Spousal Homicide." *Juristat Bulletin of the Canadian Centre for Justice Statistics,* Statistics Canada, 14, no. 8:1-15.

Wisdon, C. S. 1992. "The Cycle of Violence," National Institute of Justice, 1992.

———. 1996. "The Cycle of Violence Revisited." National Institute of Justice Research Preview, February. Typescript.

World Association for Christian Communication. 1998. *Action: News from the World Association for Christian Communication,* no. 204, March.

World Bank. 1993. *World Development Report 1993: Investing in Health.* New York: Oxford University Press.

World Health Organization. 1994. *Violence Against Women.* Geneva: WHO.

———. 1996. *"Female Genital Mutilation."* Document WHO/FRH/WHD/96.26. Geneva: WHO.

Wulf, D. 1994. *Refugee Women and Reproductive Health: Reassessing Priorities.* New York: Women's Commission for Refugee Women and Children.

Zabelina, T. 1996. "Sexual Violence Towards Women." In *Gender, Generation and Identity in Contemporary Russia,* ed. H. Pilkington. London: Routledge.

Zapata, B. C., et al. 1992. "The Influence of Social and Political Violence on the Risk of Pregnancy Complications." *American Journal of Public Health* 82, no. 5:685-90.

Zwi, A., and A. Ugalde, 1989. "Towards an Epidemiology of Political Violence in the Third World." *Social Science and Medicine* 28, no. 7:649-57.

Internet Sources

<www.adventist.org/beliefs/main_stat2.html>. 1995. *What we Believe.* Utrecht, Netherlands: Seventh-Day Adventist Church, June-July.

<www.albany.edu/sourcebook/1995/pdf/t339.pdf>. 1997. *Sourcebook of Criminal Justice Statistics.*

<www.ama-assn.org/ad-com/releases/1996/fvfact.htm>. 1996. "Facts About Family Violence: Domestic Violence." *Advocacy & Communications,* May.

<www.amnesty.org/ailib/intcam/afgan/afg1.htm>. 1995. "Women in Afghanistan: A Human Rights Catastrophe." London: Amnesty International.

<www.aph.gov.au/library/pubs/rp/1995-96/96rp27.htm>. 1995-1996. Seth-Purdie, R. "Domestic Violence: In Search of Well-Informed Policy." Department of the Parliamentary Library Research Paper 27.

<www.asksam.com/cgi-bin/as_web.exe?cavnet1+D+56209>. "Statistics on Violence Against Women." Summary of resources available.

<www.barna.org>. Barna Research Group. December.

<www.cabinet-office.gov.uk/womens-unit/1998/factsheet/6vaw.htm>. 1998. "Violence

Against Women: Why the Government Has Made Violence Against Women a Priority." U.K. Cabinet Office Fact Sheet.

<www.cdc.gov/ncipc/factsheets/ipvfacts.htm>. "Intimate Partner Violence Fact Sheet." Atlanta: Centers for Disease Control and Prevention, National Center for Injury Prevention and Control.

<www.chebucto.ns.ca/CommunitySupport/CHPNA/story10.html>. "Addressing Violence Against Women in the Black Community." Community Health Promotion Network Atlantic.

<www.china.org.cn/BeijingReview/98Jan/98-3-12.html>. "Rise in Family Violence Concerns Experts."

<www.cmwf.org/programs/women/ksc_whsurvey99_fact4_332.asp>. 1999. *Violence and Abuse*. Fact Sheet. Commonwealth Fund 1998 Survey of Women's Health, May.

<www.domesticviolencedata.org/facts/factsheets/f_esrc.htm>. 1998. "Domestic Violence, October 1998 Fact Sheet." U.K.: Economic and Social Research Council.

<www.famvi.com/dv_facts.htm>. "Myths and Facts about Domestic Violence."

<www.famvi.com/deptjust.htm>. 1995. "Women Usually Victimized by Offenders They Know." U.S. Department of Justice, August 16.

<www.fvpf.org/global/gf_china.html>. Zia, H. "China: The Other Half of the Sky."

<www.gallup.com/poll/releases/pr971025.asp>. 1997. "Many Women Cite Spousal Abuse; Job Performance Affected." Gallup News Service, October 25.

<www.ias.org.uk/alert/96issue3/violentcrime.htm>. 1996. "UK Alcohol Alert." Institute of Alcohol Studies.

<www.igc.org/iwraw/publications/countries/peru.html>. 1995. IWRAW Country Reports: Peru, September 27.

<www.infoxchange.net.au/wise/DVIM/DVFigs.htm.> 1998. *Domestic Violence Information Manual: Facts and Figures*. Women's Issues and Social Empowerment,.

<www.irlgov.ie/justice/Speeches/Speeches-99/sp2104.htm>. 1999. Speech by Mr. John O'Donoghue, T.D., Minister for Justice, Equality and Law Reform, at the Launch of Research into Domestic Violence and the Enforcement of the Law in Ireland. Dublin Castle, April 21.

<www.irlgov.ie/ag/STATUTES/96001000.htm>. 1996. *Domestic Violence Act*.

<www.irlgov.ie/garda/statistics/1997/Dviol97.htm>. 1997. "Domestic Violence Incidents 1997."

<www.igc.org/iwraw/publications/countries/peru.html>. 1995. Peru: Combined Third and Fourth Periodic Reports, September 27.

<www.jhuccp.org/pr/111/111tables.stm>. 1999. "Tables, Population Reports," series L, no. 11." *Issues in World Health* 27, no. 4 (December).

<www.jhuccp.org/popline/psm/feb00.stm>.

<www.jhuccp.org/pr/j45/j45chap3.stm>. 1996. "Reproductive Health Care: Population Reports." *Issues in World Health* 24, no. 3.

<www.jhuccp.org/pr/j46/j46chap2%5F4.stm>. 1998. "Ending Violence Against Women: Population Reports," series J, no. 46. *Issues in World Health* 26, no. 2.

<www.jhuccp.org/pr/111/111boxes.stm>. 1996. "Population Reports Side-Bars," series J, no. 46. *Issues in World Health* 24, no. 3.

<www.kw.igs.net/~bbidgood/fv.htm>. 1991. Bidgood, B., L. Tutty and M. Rothery. *An Evaluation of the Co-ordinated Family Violence Treatment Program in the Waterloo Area: A Summary Report*. Waterloo: Centre for Social Welfare Studies, University of Water-

loo.
<www.latimes.com/news/state/20000311/t000023448.html>. Ramirez, M. "A Life Saving Mission."

<www.lcweb2.loc.gov/cgi-bin/query/D?cstdy:3. 1996>. "Russia: The Role of Women."

<www.mincava.umn.edu/intnatl.asp>. International connections.

<www.mwlusa.org/pub_violence.shtml>. 1995. "An Islamic Perspective on Violence Against Women." Muslim Women's League, March.

<www.ncjrs.org/txtfiles/172837.txt>. 1998. Tjaden, Patricia, and Nancy Thoennes. *Prevalence, Incidence and Consequences of Violence Against Women: Findings from the National Violence Against Women Survey.* U.S. Department of Justice, Office of Justice Programs, National Institute of Justice and Centers for Disease Control and Prevention, November.

<www.ncadv.org/problem.htm>. "The Problem." National Coalition Against Domestic Violence.

<www.ncjrs.org/pdfiles/intimate.pdf.> 1994. "Violence Between Intimates." U.S. Department of Justice, Bureau of Justice Statistics, Selected Findings. Office of Justice Programs, November.

<www.ni.gov.uk/press/991006a-ded.htm>. 1999. "Women Tell Government They Want Choice." Northern Ireland Information Service, October 6.

<www.ni.gov.uk/press/981214d-nio.htm>. 1998. "Domestic Violence at Top of Governments Agenda for Action, Says Dr. Mowlam." Northern Ireland Information Service, December 14.

<www.ojp.usdoj.gov/bjs/pub/press/ac.pr>. 1998. "Four in Ten Criminal Offenders Report Alcohol as a Factor in Violence." U.S. Department of Justice, April 5.

<www.ojp.usdoj.gov/bhjs/pub/press/vi.pr>. 1998. "Murder by Intimates Declined 36 Percent Since 1976: Decrease Greater for Male Than for Female Victims." U.S. Department of Justice, March 16.

<www.ojp.usdoj.gov/bjs/pub/press/fvvc.pr>. 1996. "Women Are Violent Crime Victims at a Lower Rate than Men, but the Difference Is Narrowing: Women Are More Likely to Be Attacked by Intimates." U.S. Department of Justice, December 18, 1996.

<www.ojp.usdoj.gov/bjs/pub/pdf/femvied.pdf>. 1995. "Violence Against Women: Estimates from a Redesigned Survey." U.S. Department of Justice, Bureau of Justice Statistics Special Report, National Crime Victimization Survey. Office of Justice Programs, August.

<www.ojp.usdoj.gov/bjs/pub/ascii/femvied.txt>. Research on violence against women.

<www.ojp.usdoj.gov/bjs/ijs.htm>. "International Justice Statistics." U.S. Department of Justice, Bureau of Justice Statistics.

<www.saartjie.co.za/march2000/vaw14.htm>. 2000. Jelen, M. "True Rates of Family Violence in Latin America Revealed." March 14.

<www.scotland.gov.uk/news/releas98_3/pr2704.htm>. 1998. *Domestic Abuse—There Is No Excuse.* Scottish Office, December 22.

<www.scotland.gov.uk/library/documents-w3/pvaw-00.htm>. 1998. *Preventing Violence Against Women: A Scottish Office Action Plan.* Scottish Office.

<www.snbw.org/faith.htm>. 1999. *Lifeline: Support Network for Battered Women's Newsletter* 19, no. 2 (winter).

<www.un.org/rights/dpi1772e.htm>. 1996. *Women and Violence.* DPI/1771/HRB. United

Nations Department of Public Information (February).

<www.unb.ca/arts/CFVR. Research on family violence. Fredericton, N.B.: Muriel McQueen Ferguson Centre for Family Violence Research.

<www.uncjin.org/Special/GlobalReport.html>. 1999. Newman, G., ed. Excerpts from *Global Report on Crime and Justice*. New York: United Nations Office for Drug Control and Crime Prevention.

<www.unicef.org/pon97/women1.htm>. Bunch, C. "The Intolerable Status Quo: Violence Against Women and Girls." *Women Commentary*.

<www.unifem.undp.org/resour.htm>. Resources sheet. New York: United Nations Development Fund for Women.

<www.vaw.umn.edu/Documents/faith.htm>. 1998. "What Every Congregation Needs to Know About Domestic Violence: Information for Clergy, Members of Congregations, Battered Women's Programs and Human Service Providers." Seattle: Center for the Prevention of Sexual and Domestic Violence.

<www.vaw.umn.edu/vawnet/incidenc.htm>. *Incidence Rates of Violence Against Women: A Comparison of the Redesigned National Crime Victimization Survey and the 1985 National Family Violence Survey.*

<http://home.vicnet.net.au/~dvirc/Statistics.htm>. 1996. "Australian Statistics on Domestic Violence." Domestic Violence and Incest Resource Centre (DVIRC).

<www.wa.gov.au/wpdo/dvpu/actionpln.html>. 1995. "It's Not Just a Domestic." Western Australia Family and Domestic Violence Taskforce, July.

<www.wa.gov.au/wpdo/dvpu/append.html>. 1995. "Appendix 4 : A Whole Healing Approach to Violence: Aboriginal Women's Approach to Family Violence. Meeting between Aboriginal Community Women and the State Government Family and Domestic Violence Task Force and the Restraining Order Review Reference Committee, May 22-25. Sponsored by the Aboriginal Task Force and the Aboriginal Justice Council.

<www.wave-network.org/articles/111.htm>. 1998. Verein osterreichische Frauenhauser, "The Austrian Women's Shelter."

<www.wave-network.org/articles/130.htm>. 1998. Hubic, Meliha. "Statistics, Research and Campaigns" (Bosnia-Herzegovina).

<www.wave-network.org/articles/155.htm>. Estimates on the extent of male violence (Croatia).

<www.wave-network.org/articles/165.htm>. 1998. Austrian Ministry of the Interior Conference of Experts, Police Combating Violence Against Women. "Statistical Material and Governmental Reports" (Denmark).

<www.wave-network.org/articles/188.htm>. 1995. Kellegher and Associates and Monica O'Connor. "Making the Links" (Ireland).

<www.wave-network.org/articles/219.htm>. Cases of rape and domestic violence (Finland).

<www.wave-network.org/articles/220.htm>. 1998. Heiskanen, M., and M. Piispa, "Faith, Hope, Battering: A National Survey on Men's Violence Against Women in Finland." Statistics Finland.

<www.wave-network.org/articles/246.htm>. Women's Aid Federation England: "Women's Aid Annual Report 1996-97—Facts About Domestic Violence."

<www.wave-network.org/articles/274.htm>. 1995. Department of Health and Social Services, Northern Ireland Office: "Tackling Domestic Violence. A Policy for

Northern Ireland." Statistics on domestic violence.

<www.wave-network.org/articles/276.htm>. Northern Ireland Women's Aid Federation. "Statistical Report 1997/98."

<www.wave-network.org/articles/279.htm>. 1998. Royal Ulster Constabulary. Statistics on Domestic Violence, January-March (Northern Ireland).

<www.wave-network.org/articles/315.htm>. Statistical data (France).

<www.wave-network.org/articles/316.htm>. 1998. Austrian Ministry of the Interior Conference of Experts, Police Combating Violence Against Women. "Statistics on Domestic Violence in General" (France).

<www.wave-network.org/articles/339.htm>. Research on domestic violence (Hungary).

<www.wave-network.org/articles/340.htm>. Statistics almost non-existent. (Hungary).

<www.wave-network.org/articles/359.htm>. Governmental and NGO research projects (Iceland).

<www.wave-network.org/articles/360.htm>. Statistics of women's shelters (Iceland).

<www.wave-network.org/articles/370.htm>. No national surveys (Lithuania).

<www.wave-network.org/articles/378.htm>. Ministere de la Promotion Feminine. "Rapport d'activité" 1997 Annual Police Statistics" (Luxembourg).

<www.wave-network.org/articles/394.htm>. 1995. Ministry of the Presidency of the Government, General Secretary for Equality. "National Report of Greece," September.

<www.wave-network.org/articles/395.htm>. Austrian Ministry of the Interior Conference of Experts, Police Combating Violence Against Women. "No Statistics on Violence" (Greece).

<www.wave-network.org/articles/409.htm>. Micka, Elisabeth. "Statistics on Domestic Violence." Oosterbeek: De Paula Counselling Centre (Netherlands).

<www.wave-network.org/articles/429.htm>. 1998. Ministry of Children and Family Affairs, Gender Equality Division. "No Comprehensive Statistics on Domestic Violence" (Norway).

<www.wave-network.org/articles/440.htm>. 1998. Nowakowska, Urszula. "Official Data and Its Limitations." Warsaw: Centrum Praw Kobiet.

<www.wave-network.org/articles/443.htm>. 1998. Nowakowska, Urszula. "Statistics on the Criminal Justice System." Warsaw: Centrum Praw Kobiet.

<www.wave-network.org/articles/455.htm>. Reported crimes in 1987 (Portugal).

<www.wave-network.org/articles/456.htm>. 1998. Austrian Ministry of the Interior Conference of Experts, Police Combating Violence Against Women, "Statistics of the Police" (Portugal).

<www.wave-network.org/articles/485.htm>. Domestic violence against women (Romania).

<www.wave-network.org/articles/486.htm>. Domestic Violence in Eastern Europe Project/Minnesota Advocates for Human Rights. "Bucharest Forensic Hospital Data," from "Lifting the Last Curtain: A Report on Domestic Violence in Romania."

<www.wave-network.org/articles/508.htm>. Women's Organisation of the City of Skopje. Report of the Work of the SOS Line for Women and Children as Victims of Violence for the Period of 1 August 1996 to 1 August 1997. "Statistics of the SOS-Telephone" (Macedonia).

<www.wave-network.org/articles/528.htm>. Russian Association of Crisis Centres for Women. "Violence Against Women in Russia: Research, Education and Advocacy Project (REAP)."

<www.wave-network.org/articles/529.htm>. Berezjnaya, N. "Stop Violence Against Women, Campaign Russia 1998." Statistics from the Ministry for the Interior (Russia).

<www.wave-network.org/articles/547.htm>. 1998. Women's Support Project, Glasgow, Scotland. "Violence Against Women and Children. The Extent of the Problem in Scotland." Domestic violence criminal statistics.

<www.wave-network.org/articles/561.htm>. "No Serious and Valuable Research" (Slovenia).

<www.wave-network.org/articles/577.htm>. "Comment of the NGOs on Spanish Statistics" (Spain).

<www.wave-network.org/articles/578.htm>. Statistics compiled by the Instituto de la Mujer (Spain).

<www.wave-network.org/articles/588htm>. 1996. "ROKS Statistics." National Organisation of Battered Women's Shelters in Sweden.

<www.wave-network.org/articles/589htm>. "Current Statistics on Assault." Extract from Government Bill 1997/98, Violence Against Women, Ministry of Labour (Sweden).

<www.wave-network.org/articles/601.htm>. "Campaign 'Stop Violence' Final Report" (Switzerland).

<www.wave-network.org/articles/602.htm>. "Intervention of the Police" (Switzerland).

<www.wave-network.org/articles/662.htm>. 1999. Peele, H., et al. "To Live with(out) Violence: Final Report—Zenica, Bosnia-Herzegovina," April.

<www.wave-network.org/articles/675.htm>. 1998. ESRC Violence Research Programme. "Taking Stock: Statistics on Domestic Violence," Uxbridge, Middlesex: Brunel University (England).

<www.weaveinc.org/facts.html>. Facts about domestic violence and sexual assault (United States).

<www.who.dk/cpa/pr97/pr9710e.htm>. 1997. "Working Together to Stop Violence Against Women." Copenhagen: World Health Organization, August.

<www.who.dk/policy/women.htm>. 1994. "Vienna Statement on Investing in Women's Health in the Countries of Central and Eastern Europe." World Health Organization, "Women's Health Counts" Conference on the Health of Women in Central and Eastern Europe, Vienna, February.

<www.who.int/eha/wha49-25.htm>. 1996. *Prevention of Violence: A Public Health Priority.* WHA49.25. Forty-ninth World Health Assembly, May.

<http://who.int/frh-whd/publications/p-vaw1.htm>. 1997. "Report of the Meeting on the Role of the Health Sector in Violence Against Women." Copenhagen, August.

<www.who.int/frh-whd/publications/p-vaw2.htm>. 1998. "Elimination of Violence Against Women: In Search of Solutions." Geneva: World Health Organization.

<www.who.int/frh-whd/VAW/infopack/English/VAW_infopack.htm>. 1997. "Violence Against Women Information Pack: A Priority Health Issue." World Health Organization, July.

<www.who.int/frh-whd/WHD/activities/whd-vaw.htm>. "WHO Activities to End Violence Against Women."

<www.who.int/hrp/progress/47/08.html>. 1998. "Violence Against Women." Progress in Human Reproduction Research 47. Geneva: World Health Organization.

<www.who.int./inf-fs/en/fact128.html>. 1996. "Violence Against Women: Fact Sheets." World Health Organization, August.

<www.who.int/violence_injury_prevention/pages/who_prevalence_of_physical_viole.htm>. Worldwide data on violence.

<www.womensaid.org.uk/stats/statinci.htm>. Incidence of domestic violence (Britain).

<www.womensaid.org.uk/starlink.htm>. Links between abuse of women and children (Britain).